Praise for
Holding Silvan: A Brief Life

THIS BOOK CLEARLY deals with a dark, difficult, and important subject. I can't imagine anyone better equipped to do full justice to such a profound human experience.

> MICHAEL CUNNINGHAM, author of *By Nightfall* and *The Hours*

I WAS SWEPT AWAY by this book. Heartfelt, heartbreaking and brave, it takes us on a fascinating ethical journey in prose that shines with Wesolowska's love for her son. I feel fortunate for the experience, as if I have held Silvan myself. I'll never forget it.

> JULIA SCHEERES, author of *Jesus Land* and *A Thousand Lives*

A TENDER, POIGNANT and courageous narrative – insightful and beautifully written.

> ABRAHAM VERGHESE, author of *Cutting for Stone*

WHEN I PICKED UP this book for the first time, my heart sank. I wondered if I could even bear to read such a sad story. And yet, within moments, I couldn't put it down. I read long into the night, unable to leave the story until I reached its at once achingly tragic and profoundly life affirming end. That the story of the death of a child is, in fact, life affirming is a tribute to Monica Wesolowska's graceful prose, her unflinching eye, and most of all her indomitable spirit. This book taught me more about a mother's love than anything I have ever read before or since.

> AYELET WALDMAN, author of *Bad Mother: A Chronicle of Maternal Crimes, Minor Calamities, and Occasional Moments of Grace*

WHEN SOMEONE WRITES about grief they also write about courage, since they survived to tell the story. The beauty and emotional integrity of *Holding Silvan* strikes me to the core. This book is brilliant.

> LIDIA YUKNAVITCH, author of *The Chronology of Water*

Library of Congress
Cataloging-in-Publication Data

Wesolowska, Monica, 1965–
Holding Silvan : a brief life / by
Monica Wesolowska.
p. cm.
ISBN 978-0-9860007-1-3

1. Wesolowska, Monica, 1965-—
    Diaries.
2. Mothers–United States–Diaries.
3. Authors–United States–Family
    relationships.
4. Newborn infants–Death.
5. Cerebrovascular disease in
    children.
6. Parental grief.

I. Title.
HQ759.W446A3 2013
362.83′9530922–dc23
[B]

2012009392

Though this book is based on notes
taken during and immediately after
the events described, the names
and characteristics of some individ-
uals have subsequently been
changed to preserve their privacy.

Hawthorne Books
& Literary Arts

9   2201 Northeast 23rd Avenue
8   3rd Floor
7   Portland, Oregon 97212
6   hawthornebooks.com
5
4   *Form*:
3   Adam McIsaac, Bklyn, NY
2   Printed in China
1   Set in Paperback

For Silvan

Holding Silvan: A Brief Life

Monica Wesolowska

HAWTHORNE BOOKS & LITERARY ARTS
Portland, Oregon | MMXIII

Introduction
Erica Jong

THERE SEEMS NO MORE LIFE-CHANGING EVENT THAN
having a child. But having a child who is destined to die must
be more life changing still. How do we let go? How do we mourn?
These are questions people have asked themselves since time
began. The internet abounds with forums about infant loss but
there are few honest memoirs chronicling that loss. When I
looked for poems about this tragic event, I found mostly greeting
card treacle. Is this one of those human events too deep for words,
too painful to see purely?

Considering how common stillbirth, miscarriage and giving
birth to damaged children are, it's strange there is not more
literature about it. In fact, current data tells us that 10-25 percent
of all clinically recognized pregnancies end in miscarriage – no
small number. And yet this experience remains largely un-
chronicled. Like the sun, it seems that death cannot be looked
at clearly. It is too blinding, too fierce.

For centuries more babies died than lived. And mothers
died giving birth. That is a part of our history we seem to want to
deny. We want to forget all the mothers of past centuries who
dreamed of nursing their infants to life and failed. That used to
be an ordinary story. The fact that it is now extraordinary is only
due to the recent triumphs of maternal and neonatal medicine.
Some scholars have hypothesized that *Frankenstein* by Mary
Shelley is a dream of reanimation invented by an author whose

mother died a few days after her birth and many of whose infants died. Mary Shelley said the idea for the book came to her in a dream. The passionate pursuit of defeating death through science became the most enduring myth given us by a woman author. The Frankenstein myth undergoes endless permutations yet will not die. It shows us how deep our wish for denying death can be.

Holding Silvan is a memoir that takes us through all the stages of giving birth: hope, exultation, triumph. Then it becomes a meditation on loss. It is a book that takes us day by day, step by step, breath by breath through the process of letting go. It teaches us the geography of mourning. It is an unsparing almanac of grief.

Monica Wesolowska discovers how hard it is for her friends and family to even utter the verb "die". She takes us back to her childhood fear of losing her mother and how she tempted fate and tried to fool her dread by uttering the thing that she feared most. Sometimes we have to grab our fears by the scruff of the neck and tug. Only then can we domesticate our fears – like a cat.

We have never needed this book more. It comes as a rejoinder to all the superficial celebrations of childbirth that leave out its history and deny its meaning. How do you let go of a child you hoped to welcome day-by-day, breath-by-breath? Wesolowska tells that terrible story with utter simplicity and courage. It reminded me of the story of a mother dolphin carrying her dead calf on her back until finally she was ready to let it go. Giving birth brings out all our deepest mammalian feelings: the need to nurture, to protect, to heal – even when we have given up hope.

The hardest part of this book – for both author and reader – is Silvan's lingering, neither wholly alive nor wholly dead. I marveled at Wesolowska's endurance. I marveled at her transparent prose that was backlit with the deepest emotions, starting with love. This is truly the hardest kind of writing, and the most rewarding to any reader. It must have been excruciating to endure this passage and more excruciating still to memorialize it in words. All writers know that writing is not always catharsis. A door has been opened not closed. I hope *Holding Silvan* will inspire other writers to tell the truth about this passage.

I have always believed that children drag us into adulthood. Here, indeed, is further proof.

Contents

HOLDING SILVAN: *a brief life*

Hope is not the conviction that something will turn out well
but the certainty that something makes sense, regardless of how
it turns out.

VÁCLAV HAVEL

You'll never know, dear,
How much I love you.
Please don't take my Silvan away.

VARIATION ON "YOU ARE MY SUNSHINE"

Birth

IN THE MORNING, THE PHONE NEXT TO MY HOSPITAL bed rings. Stepping from the shower, my skin scrubbed of the sweat and blood of yesterday's triumphant labor, I slip past David to pull on my old robe and head for the phone. I'm not worried. I'm expecting another friend, a relative, more words of congratulation to match my sudden pleasure in my baby – a healthy, full-term boy who waits for me in the nursery – but the woman on the other end of the line is a stranger.

"Hello, darling," the stranger says in a husky, soothing voice. She is calling from another hospital. She says she needs to clear up some confusion about the spelling of my name before the transfer. I, too, am confused. When I tell the stranger that I don't understand, that I am about to go down the hall to collect my baby because it's time to nurse, she says, "I'm so sorry to be the one to tell you, darling."

With these vague but tender words, the ecstatic glow of motherhood that has surrounded me since Silvan's birth begins to fade.

An ambulance waits; the transfer is happening any minute. Wrapped still in my dirty robe with its stiff patch of dried blood in back, I open the bathroom door and try to convey the stranger's words to David hidden in the steam. Though David has told me his worries about Silvan since the birth, I've dismissed them all as mere symptoms of new fatherhood.

"Wait for me," he says turning off the water, but there is no way.

If I could, I would fly to my son.

IN THE NURSERY, five people stand around Silvan's bed. Five people. This is the baby's "transport team" as someone puts it – two people to wheel the bed, one to drive, two more "just in case." In case of what? In the night, when the resident had taken Silvan from me because he would not stop crying – mewls like a kitten, peeps like a bird – she only wanted me to sleep. She'd promised to bring him back when it was time to nurse. Even when she returned a few hours later to tell me they needed to keep Silvan for "observation," I hadn't begun to worry. I was too tired, too happy. I'd roused myself to go down to the nursery to see what they were worried about – cute little fist curls they called seizures. I'd held Silvan until I thought I'd pass out, then returned to bed without him. Nine months of hope is a hard habit to break. Besides, even if they were right in the night, he is totally calm now, sleeping peacefully. At last, he has stopped crying. Surely this is a good sign?

"It's the phenobarbital," they say.

I would stay beside his bed until they've wheeled him off to the ambulance, but a nurse comes in. She's been searching for me, racing around coordinating my discharge. She needs me back in my room for an exam by a midwife. There's paperwork to do, a birth certificate to apply for, milk to pump. She's helpful but unpleasant. "Do you want to be discharged now or not? Because I have all my ducks in a row."

Back in our room, my mother has arrived; David's father and stepmother, too. I call out to them how cute the baby is – "just like David" – as they are ushered into the hall. The midwife spreads my legs. The breast pump arrives and I insert one breast into each cup, sign a birth certificate, agree to a home visit from a nurse and who knows what else, while the breast pump makes its thump and suck. Hospital staff tells me not to be embarrassed, they've seen it all before. David is searching the room for our possessions, which he stuffs into clear plastic bags provided by the hospital. The only thing he can't find is the charger for his cellphone. It seems a small detail, too small to mention, but the symbolism is clear: soon we will become almost impossible to reach.

"HELLO MOM. HELLO Dad." Shelley, the husky-voiced receptionist who'd called earlier, welcomes us to her hospital.

I am slow-moving but not in pain. Back at the other hospital, the last thing I'd done was put on my shoes and my mother had praised me for being able to stand on one foot so soon after birth – as if she herself is not equipped with such maternal strength. But maybe the recovery of my body matters as much to her as it does to me: it seems that this is the least I deserve, a body that can recover swiftly enough to care for a baby who must have been damaged while inside of me. For even though everything about my pregnancy and labor and delivery had seemed blessed, something has obviously gone wrong.

Shelley comes around her desk to hug us.

We are entering her world, the world of the Neonatal Intensive Care Unit, the dreaded NICU, a world where parents must dress in hospital scrubs to hold their children. Shelley shows us the routine: remove watch and jewelry, push sleeves above elbow, remove sponge and nail-pick from its plastic package, turn on water by whacking the metal knee pedal, get soap by depressing the squishy foot pedal, scrub, scrub, scrub thirty seconds each side, all the way up to the elbow.

On the whiteboard behind Shelley's desk, I'm shocked to see my last name listed, proof that parenthood is not going the way I had imagined. Baby Boy Wesolowska, the whiteboard says, though our son's name is Silvan Jerome Fisher.

DR. A IS a strapping man, almost-handsome, with steady, almost-kind eyes. Almost, I say, because he is not my baby and my baby is everything in the world right now. Anything else can only be almost. Dr. A speaks to us clearly and intelligently as Silvan's neonatologist. We stand by the side of Silvan's bassinet. Unlike many of the babies in bassinets around him, Silvan is plump and whole. Still he looks odd, lying by himself under a heat lamp.

Dr. A speaks with optimism but with an honesty that admits the unknown. His first diagnosis is best-case. "We have no evidence so far of anything but what we call subdural hematoma, a blood clot under the skull." He says this happens sometimes during labor. After all, he reminds me that I pushed for several hours to get the baby around my pubic bone. Pushing for several hours is not uncommon with a first baby, but it's not ideal. He holds up his hands to show us the plates of a baby's head, and how they are still mobile, moving like continents. They are supposed to be this way, but sometimes when they crunch together in the birth canal they cause bleeding which leaves clots. These clots will shrink with time.

"This may cause seizures for him later in life, or it may not."

With motherly pride, I assume it will not. And if it does, well, people live with seizures. My father, after whom Silvan has taken his middle name Jerome, had two seizures in his twenties. Though the seizures alarmed and embarrassed him, he went on to marry, have four children and a significant career.

And yet, as I hear the news, I feel faint. I say, "I have to sit." And then I add, "It's not because of what you're saying." Already, I know it's important for this man to know that he can speak to me straight, that I don't need to be coddled. I like honesty. But I do feel sick, woozy, and nauseated. Perhaps it's a postpartum hot flash. "I just gave birth," I remind him, apologetic, as some- one wheels a stool my way.

THE NURSES TAKE over for a while. One brings me a little square of flannel. "Tuck this inside your bra or somewhere close to your skin and wear it for a day, then bring it back. We'll put it by your baby's nose so he can smell you while you're not here. That will comfort him." Another brings me bottles and shows me a room where I can pump milk.

"I know he can't nurse right now, but when he's better, we'll start with the first bottles and go on from there so he doesn't miss anything. That will also keep your own milk supply up and ready for him."

I am stunned by their solicitude. Prior to his birth, friends promoted home births to me. Hospitals, they told me, were sterile, stressful places that ignored the wisdom of a mother's body. At home, they seemed to think, nothing ever went wrong. But I liked my obstetrician, trusted her to trust me to give birth naturally. And I'd succeeded. For sixteen hours, I'd imagined ocean waves arriving and receding, getting high on my own endorphins as my body moved through novel pain, and then I'd pushed the baby out … but instead of being alert and drug-free, he'd been limp and silent. The triumph of that natural labor is now separating from the outcome as if the two events are unrelated. If this happened to him in a hospital, I tell myself, it could have happened anywhere. At least I'm not facing the blame for having risked a home birth; at least they're treating me well, as if I am necessary and important, as if I am his mother. Because I am his mother, even if he is not in my arms.

WE RENT A breast pump to take home. That first night without him, I wake myself every few hours as if I have a newborn waking me, and sit in the dark living room, open my robe and put the suction cups on; the industrial-strength whirr and thump begins, the milk flows, my womb cramps as it's supposed to do in the early days of nursing, and I cry. My sobs mingle with the whirr and thump until David distinguishes the human from the machine and leaps from bed to wrap his arms around me.

Over and over David leaps from whatever he is doing, sleeping, eating, talking on the phone, to comfort me, in the shower, over breakfast, in the car. He stops what he's doing and focuses on me. He's the one who returns phone calls, tells neighbors the news while I huddle over nothing in the car. He finds us gowns to put on at the hospital, gets us glasses of water to drink at Silvan's bedside. He tends to me so I can tend to our son. He's always been good at tending to me. Ever since we met, I've known I could rely on him. This time, he hasn't stopped moving since my water broke and he rushed around the house, putting dishes in the sink, packing my toothbrush, timing my contractions until – minutes later, it seemed, though David says it was an hour – it was time, I put on my old brown corduroy coat that strained at its buttons, and we went off to the hospital together.

EXCEPT TO SLEEP, we hardly leave the hospital for the next few days. For hours and hours we are out of contact with everyone but immediate family – David's father and stepmother, my mother, my brother and his girlfriend, David's sister and her boyfriend – who gather in the hallway outside. I was already on maternity leave when I went into labor, but David has to call his boss that first morning home, and his boss tells him to forget the world of work. How grateful we feel.

Only two people are allowed at the baby's bedside at a time. We take turns bringing them in. Sometimes we let two people in together while we take a break. We break for the bathroom, for food down in the cafeteria. On the second afternoon, we actually leave the hospital for lunch while Silvan is off for a test. David thinks this is a good idea because the hospital food is so bland it's hard to eat and because it will distract us while Silvan is in other people's hands.

Going out is torture. All these people eating on their work breaks, choosing between rye and sourdough as if life itself hangs in the balance. *Just choose and eat, you fools*, I think, *because back at the hospital real life is happening*.

Indeed, on our return that day from the deli, we find ourselves holding the doors of the elevator for a baby on a gurney. We stand back against the walls, one on each side of the elevator while the baby's bed is wheeled between us. I hardly want to look. My own misfortune is enough to bear. But David says, "Look, it's Silvan."

"No it's not," I say, almost scornful, for how can he know better than me?

"Yes, it is."

"No it's not," I say with certainty, talking over the baby's bed, for when they first wheeled Silvan away after birth – "just for a few minutes" – they'd stopped to show him to me, the very baby I'd hoped for, looking not at all like me but like his handsome father: a head of dark hair, eyes ringed with heavy lashes, broad pink cheeks tapering down to fat red lips etched against the olive of his skin. When we first came to this second hospital, wasn't I the one – bursting with pride – who found him in his bassinet while David said, "But how do you know that's him?" Surely David is confused because newborns all have the same strange, squashed faces, the same upturned noses. Is it even possible for a baby who was just inside of me to be out here, unrecognizable?

"Excuse me," David says to the hospital staff who have been ignoring us, looking straight ahead. "That's Baby Boy Wesolowska, isn't it?"

They agree, but warily, as if we might be baby snatchers, or as if we've caught them wheeling our baby around the hospital for fun, or as if they've learned bad news. I can see this last possibility now, because that is how the next technician behaves a few hours later. At first she seems glad to see us arrive. Silvan is in bed, electrodes stuck all over his head, asleep. She assures us the EEG will not hurt him. She says we can help. She's very friendly, telling us how cute he is, cooing over his calm, cute body. I assume he's so quiet because of the phenobarbital he's been given since the seizures of his first night. He's always asleep. She opens her laptop. She herself grows quiet as she studies the patterns she reads there.

"Okay," she says pleasantly, "would you mind stroking him a little?"

With pleasure, I rub his chest, his arms.

"Okay," she says, "a little harder."

Still, I stroke him softly.

"Could you pinch him?"

David pinches him.

"A little harder," she says. And then, "Did you really pinch him?"

Suddenly, she closes her laptop. She refuses to make eye contact. She leaves saying nothing at all.

DESPITE OUR HOPES, the news grows worse. By the third day, we know the seizures are due to more than hematomas; they will not just go away with time. There is evidence now that Silvan has suffered some greater "insult" to his brain. We want to point out to the doctors that they are being inconsistent. We want to hold them to an earlier diagnosis, as if to a better deal advertised in that morning's paper. We want to go back to those first few minutes after birth when we thought the only thing wrong was a slight distress, a slight lethargy. We want our only disappointment to be that he could not lie on my chest right away. We want to be relieved that, after wheeling him off for those "few minutes" to aspirate his lungs, they were able to bring him back lusty and strong enough to nurse.

We would settle for that.

Instead, we have a baby who was born, who nursed and cried, but who is now in a coma – this word has been used at last – and who may die before we even know what's wrong with him. Though he seems simply, sweetly asleep, he may never revive. We wake on our third morning at home to the ringing phone. My heart hammers as David answers. But no, I can tell from his end of the conversation that the worst has not happened. Silvan has not died before I could get dressed for the day and see him again. But what David says is scary enough.

"A meeting with a neurologist?"

And, "At one o'clock?"

And then, "Can't you tell me now?"

I'm out of bed, packing a bag to take to the hospital, sanitary pads, the squirt bottle for my healing stitches. When David gets off the phone, he says, "The EEG did not look good."

"But what does that mean?" I ask.

"Brain damage?" David says as if posing a question.

I'm facing him but now my head turns away, then my torso; I am falling on the bed and all I see is a grey kaleidoscope, slowly closing on the last spot of light at the end of the tunnel: "I can't go on," I say. *This is what my mother felt*, I think, *lying at the bottom of the basement stairs after hearing that Mark's body had been found.* But, even as I have this thought, the sensation passes because I am not my mother, my son has not killed himself, my husband is not about to die, and already I can see myself from the outside, already I'm mocking myself for melodrama, because I have lived through tragedies before, and this is not a tragedy. After all, my baby is waiting.

ONE O' CLOCK. We sit side-by-side, close but not touching. I can't touch David. The situation feels too dangerous; I feel my brain crouching down, ready to spring. Intellect is how I deal. Crisis speeds my thinking. We are in an ugly room, narrow as a hallway, with a too-big table shoved inside it, a box of tissues in the middle, a blur of faces. Dr. A is there, a resident, a social worker, a nurse, half a dozen more at least. I'm not looking at them. I am looking only at the new doctor, the specialist, this neurologist, who is now in charge it seems. This is her meeting. She looks twenty-one with her smooth blond hair hanging free. She looks as if she'd been a girl who once was popular and consequently had downplayed her brains until one day it occurred to her that she didn't have to choose between looks and brains, she had enough of both to conquer the world. Here she comes, ready to conquer ours.

"The infant was transferred to this hospital after observed seizures. The initial impression was subdural hematomas…" she begins, and then the words keep coming from her, medical terms, "basal ganglia" and "thalami" and "sagittal sinus." I try to stop her. I say, "What does that mean?" but she keeps on talking as if I've said nothing. She seems to think she's addressing a panel of experts and not two parents whose need to understand is urgent. The room feels very bright. She talks about "burst suppression patterns" and "EEGs." Again, I say, "What does that mean?" but as in a dream where one cannot get the words out, she doesn't seem to hear me. At last she gets to what really matters to us. The prognosis. She says, "Physical and mental impairment." She says it unadorned like that and stops.

"Could you describe what you mean?" I ask.

For the first time, she looks at me. "It could just mean stiff limbs," she says stiffly, as if I'm forcing her to speak a language she barely knows.

"Stiff limbs is fine with me," I say.

"…and he won't be a straight A student."

"Well that is not acceptable," I say. It is my humor, my father's humor, dark, deadpan, so close to the truth it glances off it like a spear, a humor that sometimes got him into trouble when it rattled to the ground uncaught. No one reacts.

"But it could be much worse than that," she says, smooth and unsmiling.

It's hard to imagine this woman has suffered. Her children, whom she has not yet had, will, of course, get straight A's like her and I hate her for it – such is the venom of grief as it begins to spread inside me.

We go back and forth, asking questions, but she will not commit; she keeps holding out hope like little bits of candy, until I've had it. She's sugar-coating something terrible. I say something to this effect. I say I want to know what one can do for a baby whose life has been saved for a life that is not really life at all. I use the word euthanasia; I know it is illegal, I say, but what else is allowed? There is cold shock in the room. Or perhaps the shock I feel is my own. I feel it in my chest, a flutter of my heart as though I'm in danger of falling, but all I want is to move away from the slippery ice of hope to truth.

Beside me, David seems suddenly unable to sit still. He scratches his neck, his shin, he frowns, he sighs. I touch his arm: "Do you need this meeting to be over?" Though I want to press on, though I want to ply them with questions and force them in this way to tell me more than anyone can ever know about the future, though I'd rather keep pushing forward intellectually than let emotion overwhelm me, David says, "We need to be alone right now." He is about to explode with tears.

They are instantly on their feet and filing swiftly out. Their relief at having fulfilled this part of their job is palpable.

As soon as we are alone, we hug. We sob.

"Promise me, whatever happens, this won't ruin our marriage," I say, pulling away from him; and at the same time, David says, "Let's try to have another child someday, okay?" These seem like loving words; but as I record them here, I grow uncomfortable wondering if there is love enough in them for Silvan.

Love Story

ONE AFTERNOON AROUND THE TIME DAVID AND I DECIDED we were ready for children, we went for a hike in the redwoods. We'd taken our time coming to this decision. In fact, it had been my doctor who tipped the balance, bringing out statistics and showing me that if I didn't choose one way or other soon, nature would choose for me. I was already thirty-six and had been with David for nine years, married to him for two. And so we decided to try; and that afternoon after sex, we went for a hike. It was a hot, sunny day and the cool, sweet-smelling woods matched the afterglow of sex so that, as we hiked, our coupling seemed to extend and fill the day. Yellow sunlight fingered the red trunks of the trees and the spongy, decaying forest floor. We didn't expect to get pregnant, but we were ready to be pregnant when it happened.

"We should remember this day," I called to David further up the trail, "in case the day we actually conceive is less lovely." After all, we knew many couples who'd worked hard to have children. We were hiking uphill, panting with the effort. A plane passed overhead, birds rustled in the undergrowth. Now we descended, the fecund silence deepening as our breathing slowed.

"We could," David said with bemused affection.

A month later, we conceived Silvan, though I do not know exactly when. Those days have been lost in ordinary repetition. What I remember instead is sunshine filtering through trees and catching on a cloud of gnats, on swirling wood dust, the air always glittering a few steps ahead.

LONG BEFORE THAT sunny day in the woods with David, I used to tell myself another story, a story about the boy I'd someday marry. I spotted him – this future husband of mine – for the first time when I was twelve and on a pilgrimage to Lourdes that my family undertook one summer as a daytrip while we were already in France visiting my mother's relatives. The day was golden hot and a scruffy, pale boy with straight, tawny hair stood at a fountain drinking. "Drink," his parents said each time he stopped. When they heard us speaking English, they turned and asked, "Do you have aspirin? He has a headache." Never having known a child to suffer a headache before, I studied him with curiosity, his pale strained face, his flat hair. But we didn't carry aspirin and as we walked away, my mother said softly, "I didn't know children suffered headaches." She said it as if in disbelief or awe.

We were headed to the grotto, that circle of rock where the Virgin Mary appeared to Saint Bernadette. Though my parents were liberal intellectuals who would've traveled farther for a good museum, they were also solid Catholics who believed in saints and miracles. As I stood looking up at the rows of crutches from cripples who'd been miraculously healed at Lourdes, I told myself not to forget the tawny-headed boy. Someday he might become my husband. It wasn't that he was cute, or funny, or interesting. I was drawn to him solely because of his suffering.

Back home, I kept watch for future husbands. These were never boys I found attractive, only needy in some way. Loneliness especially moved me, including the loneliness of dolls left at home while I was off at school, or flies trapped on windowsills. There was one fly I kept company in the bathroom all afternoon until my mother rushed in – the wooden soles of her sandals clacking on the tiles – and swatted it. There my friend lay, six black legs up in the air, while I cried over it. "But you didn't tell me he was your friend!" my mother said before rushing off to tend to other children.

My mother had four of us to tend to, not counting the occasional foster child; I was the oldest, followed by Mark, Katya, and Kim. Though my parents had traveled far to meet each other – my father, orphaned by high school, had escaped his factory job in Wisconsin for a Ph.D. in physics; my mother, a child of the blitzkrieg of London, had escaped for her own Ph.D. in the States – in Berkeley they were determined to raise a family as Catholic as their own. In such a family, sainthood seemed a worthy occupation and so I continued to aspire to it, lying in bed, both longing for and dreading the moment when God would appear across the yellow shag of my bedroom rug. Perhaps He would ask for something so big I couldn't handle it, like lead an army, or something so small I couldn't bear it. I feared, for example, the life of Saint Monica. My mother said she was a lovely saint to have been named after, but hers sounded like no life to me. She spent it praying for the soul of her son.

While waiting for divine directive, I also practiced "good" deeds. These deeds made other people's suffering bearable to me. One day I arranged a race for a boy named Leo. Leo was two years younger than me, a boy in Mark's class. Leo was too chubby to play easily with the other kids and at recess often stood at the edges of games watching, while I sat farther out watching him watching. I assumed he was lonely; I assumed that winning a race would bring him friends. In this race, I arranged for Mark to pretend to trip so that Leo could win. Mark must have had the same deluded sense of pity as I did, a child's pity not yet developed into true compassion. The day of the race came. Though a crowd gathered when Mark fell, though I kept yelling, "Run, Leo, run," thinking his victory would be all the more satisfying for having an audience, Leo only looked confused, then went back to help Mark up. And when I crowed, "You won, you won!" anyway he did not break into a smile. He went back to his own life and I went back to mine, each of us learning to manage on our own.

When David and I first met in Berkeley, I'd long since given up my vision of marrying to assuage someone else's loneliness. And David clearly was not my tawny-haired youth at the fountain. No, David was Jewish, darkly handsome, and he'd never been to Lourdes. Not only that, he wasn't a tortured artist either, the mate I'd since imagined for myself. Instead, he was my competent superior at work; and at twenty-four, he seemed as burdened with a sense of responsibility as a middle-aged man. David for his part had always pictured a woman with a solid job. Instead, I was a twenty-eight-year-old temporary worker and aspiring writer who'd just moved back in with her parents to save money. In other words, David was as unlike all the pale, wounded, wild men I'd loved before as I was unlike all the well-groomed, well-padded women he'd dated before, and neither of us expected much from that first date.

There he stood on my parents' front porch, too eager to please, too cautious about standing out; even his curly hair was combed flat the way he'd done it throughout his New Jersey adolescence; in contrast, I wore a fluorescent paisley headscarf cut from the hem of a floor-length skirt my mother had worn during my Berkeley childhood. That scarf was so bright you could direct traffic with it and my wild hair stood up in a halo around it. After taking in my stoplight head, David came inside the house where my father was sitting in the living room. David tried to bullshit my father by pretending to know more about the writer in the movie we were going to see than he really did. He flubbed it by suggesting that my father must know the work of this writer himself, but my father said he didn't and asked David to tell him more, which David couldn't. I was embarrassed. I'd been raised to believe that the only way to learn was to admit what one doesn't know. Honesty as the path to truth.

My father was already ill by then, but he'd hauled himself up from his armchair to meet the young man taking me out on a date, and once it became clear that David was going in circles just to please him, my father sat back down heavily, told us to have a good time, and went back to staring out the window.

After the movie, I continued to be frustrated. I wanted to talk deeply about the movie and David wanted to show me the first place he'd worked on campus. So why was I falling in love? For I was falling in love. The story of our union as we tell it is one of feeling absolutely comfortable. As if we'd known each other for a long time. As we walked around town together, though I could not get him to talk about movies and books and art the way I wanted, I could get him to talk about things that mattered on a deeper level. Though he had bullshitted my father about what facts he knew, he was absolutely honest about his feelings. There was a comfortable familiarity and safety in his honesty. For example, when pressed he said he didn't find my headscarf flattering.

We also got into a conversation about God, whom David didn't believe in. Never had. He'd never believed in fairies, either, or in the lives of his sister's dolls. When I tried to explain how I'd come to understand God over time – my sense that matter is all connected, that there is more in our brains than we can understand, that we need to be humble in the face of this mystery – he said, "Why call that God?"

I thought perhaps we could agree on that point, but then he went on to say that he thought someday we might under-stand it all, that science was constantly advancing. I wasn't so sure about that. I've never understood the word progress except to mean an apparent forward motion in time. "How can you be so arrogant about being human?" I said.

"No, it's the reverse," he said. "When something bad hap-pens, I don't see the point in blaming a god. But when some-thing good happens, I do look around in gratitude, wanting to thank someone other than myself."

With the glib naïveté of youth, I told him I wouldn't want to raise a child but that I'd find giving birth an interesting experience to have as a writer, and though David didn't understand giving birth except to have a child, he did say that were we to have children and not just give birth to them, he'd want to raise them Jewish, and I said that was okay. We were speaking theoretically. We had time to change our minds. Anyway, I wasn't a practicing Catholic anymore whereas – as David explained it – one can be raised Jewish and atheist because being Jewish is more about culture than religion.

But there was a complicating factor in all of this and if I go right back to the moment when he asked me out for that first date, I can see where I fell for him. When David approached my chair at work that day, my brother Mark was already dead and my father was already feeling ill and David was just a handsome young man who'd only ever lost a grandfather. Still I liked the way, when I said that catching a movie that particular weekend might be difficult because of a memorial mass scheduled for my brother who'd killed himself nine months before, he did not flee. When I told him the mass might be cancelled because we needed the priest to come up to the house to do a "laying on of the hands" to heal my father of cancer, he still did not flee. Instead, he went down on one knee at my swivel chair, and asked me to tell him more. He looked me full in the eyes. He said, "That must be hard."

He was a rational skeptic, and a young man, but he knew how to listen. He listened as I tried to describe grief. He listened as I tried to describe my sense of something greater than ourselves, a sense of our souls returning to some mysterious whole. He listened as if he understood that it did not matter what I believed about death so long as I believed in something. No, it wasn't that. He listened as if by listening he could make my suffering easier to bear.

Making This Easier

"WHAT WILL MAKE THIS EASIER FOR YOU?" DAVID
asks.

We are lying in bed on the fourth morning after Silvan's
birth. We feel as if we have not stopped moving since my water
broke during dinner, and our minds are swirling with
diagnoses and prognoses. The doctors now know that Silvan
suffered oxygen deprivation. They know this insult to his brain
happened during labor or delivery, but they don't know exactly
when or how. I wish I could help, but when I think back to my
labor, those sixteen hours, everything seemed normal and
natural. My water breaking, tickling my legs, the contractions
starting within minutes; the drive to the hospital, my water
clear, the baby fine; walking the hospital halls, sitting on a birthing ball, picturing the push and pull of ocean waves, dozing
between each contraction; and though I'd felt in the grip of
something powerful and mysterious, I'd felt confident. Only
once did my confidence waver, when I woke to see that David
had left his post by my bed. "What are you doing?" I asked in
alarm as if I could not survive the next contraction without him.

"I'm just putting on my shoes."

"Where are you going?"

"Nowhere. My feet are cold."

The nursing notes corroborate this picture: "husband and
doula are supportive," the notes say; and I am laboring "well."

Now the doctors continue to analyze this simple narrative. I wore a fetal monitor strapped around my belly to monitor the baby's heart rate. This is standard practice, an attempt to catch distress such as Silvan was in. I know that some of my friends who labored at home are skeptical of hospital monitoring. They believe that midwives do a better, more human job of monitoring, and yet one of these friends now remembers a story of a homebirth ending in an inexplicable stillbirth. Now the doctors go back to the monitor tracings, but they find nothing unusual. When I admit that I had hated the feel of the monitor belt around my belly so much that I had begged the nurses to take it off—there it is, a gap of two hours in the nursing notes while I stand in the shower—the doctors say that for a normal labor like mine, they usually monitor intermittently anyway. Nor do they know what to say about the last kick I felt in the shower, a big kick as if Silvan were stretching out inside of me with all his strength. A baby's kick is usually a good sign. What's strange to them instead is how the damage doesn't show up anywhere else but in Silvan. We learn about cord blood gasses and placentas, neither of which showed signs of damage. Nor did the tests right after birth show much more than lethargy. All they know for sure is that the damage happened during labor, because the brain swells within twenty-four hours of such an injury. Perhaps this is why, though he nursed, he could not stop crying. Because something unseen was already wrong.

BUT NONE OF this is enough to make sense of what is happening. No medical information can. There's something else I need—and when David asks in bed what will make this easier, I know what it is. "I want people to see him, my baby," I say. In that moment, the miracle of Silvan is that he is mine, that he came out of me, and I am flooded with a maternal pride of possession.

We begin by inviting Margie and Gavin. David has known

these two since college, since before they were a couple, and I have known them since I met David, right before they fell in love. They seem entwined with us as a couple. We've taken swing dancing lessons with them (David dropping Margie on her head), vacationed with them, we've planned our weddings together, and nine months before us, they gave birth to their own first child. Nine months before, we'd gone off eagerly to see Margie and Gavin and their newborn son Oscar, and after David saw Margie, still swollen and exhausted but rushing around full of her characteristic glee and good humor with a babe in arms, David said to me with his usual blunt honesty, "I can't really picture you having what it takes to be a mother." We were approaching a curve on the freeway when he said this, me at the wheel, and I felt enraged. This was the same curve where I'd felt myself losing control six years before (a late driver, I was taught by David) and he had reached over calmly to put a steady hand on the wheel. This time, our roles were reversed. In that moment on the freeway, I knew I was pregnant. While he anxiously reminded me that I was a writer and that writing was selfish, I felt already changed. I felt equal to this rushing curve ahead. "I'm going to be a mother," I said, rounding the curve with competence, "with you or without you." Already the hormones were kicking in, making me this angry, this weepy, this full of my own defiant sense of power. In this state, David's familiar honesty felt intolerable. He asked how I could be so certain I was pregnant. "I just know," I said, "so you'd better practice saying only nice things to me from now on." He grinned. We were getting off the freeway now, both of us grinning, and I let go of the steering wheel for a moment to take his hand as if I'd been driving this well all my life.

When we arrive at the hospital, Margie and Gavin are already waiting for us in the hall. Oscar is not with them and for a moment, I am hugely disappointed. I had wanted this spark of life and hope. But Margie says her sister-in-law thought it would be better for me if I didn't have to deal with someone else's child. And I realize she is probably right. They have dropped everything, including Oscar, for this moment with us.

David takes Gavin in to see Silvan while Margie and I go into the little waiting room. It is dark and done in beige, and covered with blankets and pillows and crumpled magazines from all the parents who've camped out the night before. It is ugly and grim.

I try to explain to Margie what little I know in a hushed voice so I don't disturb the woman a few chairs down with her swollen face and eyes tilted vacantly up at the TV. She has just come from the Bad News Room, as we now call that room where we met with the neurologist, so I know she's a fellow sufferer. Now I have to tell Margie how bad the situation is, how this is not something that Silvan will recover from after a few days in hospital the way the babies of friends have always recovered until now. "He was perfectly healthy," I say. "I had a natural labor, it all seemed totally fine. He came out looking perfect to me."

"So what happened?" she asks.

"They don't know. He's got severe hypoxic ischemic encephalopathy," I say, stumbling over the words, "which basically means he was deprived of oxygen for long enough that his central nervous system was damaged. Maybe there was a clot in his placenta. Or a clot in him. Or maybe he grabbed his own umbilical cord so hard he killed his own brain."

"A baby can do that?"

"A really strong baby, I guess. He's very healthy. They keep telling me how healthy he is. His lungs. His heart. They say I took really good care of him in utero." I look over at the woman watching TV. She isn't listening to us, but it is too awful, too much like the death of my brother Mark, this inexplicable death by asphyxiation, as if my healthy son has chosen to hang himself. Relatives of the woman watching TV look in through the doorway at Margie and me, then beckon the woman out into the hallway where they huddle miserably under the fall of bright lights to confer. We are left blessedly alone in the dim, stagnant room.

I tell Margie what else I don't know. I tell her that in most cases of severe asphyxia the exact time and cause are never determined. I tell her that, though pregnant women are told that asphyxia "never happens" anymore, it still happens to varying degrees in ten percent of all births. Then I tell her about the range that the neurologist has given us. It is this that is the worst. "He might be so damaged he can't breathe on his own, or he might be only mildly retarded. He might die in a few days, or he might live with us until we die. And David's freaking out on me." This is the first time I talk to someone about how David and I are doing. Since the moment David saw Silvan across the delivery room from me, so like a dying patient surrounded with equipment and doctors, David has been suffering. Now he wants answers. He needs to understand so that he can act. In his anxiety to know what the future holds, we no longer seem to be handling the speed of this car together but have rounded that curve on the highway to find a wall. Our differences are coming out, his desire for certainty and my tolerance of mystery are clashing. "What if my marriage can't survive this?"

Margie goes down on one knee by my chair. Her voice is very low and intimate. "I want you to know that no matter what happens," she says, "we are here for you and David, and that if you have a brain-damaged child, I will love him and my child will love him, I will make my children be Silvan's friend and we will treat him as part of our family." Margie is from a big, Catholic family, thirteen children; she knows about family obligation. For a moment, there is no one in the world but us carried along by the force of her speech which is so beautiful and passionate and nearly impossible.

"But you can't force someone to love someone else," I finally say.

"I know," she says, tears coming.

My tears come too. I sob, sobbing almost with relief that

we can cry like this together, this friend whom I've known only in good times. The most serious conversation I can remember having had with her until this moment is about her unexpected desire to give her child a Catholic baptism even though she no longer practices any religion. "Anyway, he might not even survive," I say now.

"Would it be better for him to die on his own?"

How relieved I am that she is someone who can use that word "die." How hard to use that word in conjunction with a baby. How wrong in a world where most babies survive. But I am beginning to suspect that he has been trying to do just that since the moment of his birth. To die. I nod.

She says, "That feels so strange to hope for."

I Hope Mommy Dies

WHEN I WAS VERY YOUNG, WALKING UP THE HILL TOWARD home after school, or lying in my narrow bed at night, I would think, "I hope Mommy dies." With these words, I tried to relieve the pressure of my dread, to speak the unspeakable, that primal fear, the starting point of fairytales. I wanted to trick whoever might be listening: a god, a genie. I wanted to be spared that inevitable loss by pretending not to care. But there must have been fascination, too; for though my mother remained mercifully alive, I hoarded other deaths. I spent time with my fly, his upside-down legs in the air; I collected the shells left behind by snails starting with the big, understandable ones and working down to a shell as small and translucent as a baby's fingernail. It seemed somehow important to do this, to pay attention to death, as if I could grow into the deaths that would be most painful.

The first human death in my life was remote. It happened to an old man named Maurice in a bank in England. Uncle Maurice as I called him was not really my uncle, nor did I know him well, but a few months before he died I had spent a week with my mother and my youngest brother Kim in England at the flat of my grandmother Chmum. Maurice was Chmum's good friend, tall and stooped and very bald. From these simple features, I recognized him again years later in a photo album in France. My mother and I were in the apartment that Chmum had settled into in old age. We had just returned from a day spent at the nursing home where Chmum was dying, and I was pregnant.

The night before flying to France, I'd found out. "Don't tell anyone," David had said because he wanted time to adjust. So
there we were, my mother and I, in an apartment in France surrounded by someone else's possessions. The first picture album
I flipped through was a black-and-white trip around France,
after my grandparents separated, after their children were
grown-up and gone. Chmum and Maurice sitting on a split-rail
fence; beside their shadows wavy on a cobblestone street;
leaning against a square, black car. Their faces looked the same
day by day, but Chmum's hair changed, sometimes quite
extravagantly, in one photo its perfect waves piled up like a hat.

Thinking there must have been someone else along to
have taken so many pictures, I was pleased to find the photogra-
pher at last, first in a shadow on the ground, then standing on
the other side of Chmum. Opening a second album, I found this
man again, the same hooked nose and thick eyebrows, this time
on the edge of a crowd.

"Dédé," my mother said when I asked. Short for André.
Chmum's dead brother.

I knew André only from a smiling portrait in a round frame
that always stood on a shelf wherever Chmum lived, first in
England, then in her native France where she returned to live at
the end.

"He doesn't look so good," I said.

My mother examined the photos.

"You're right," she said. "This is his last trip to England,
right before he found out about the cancer."

He looks a little pale, a little swollen, but more than that:
whereas the rest of the party are smiling at the camera, he is
smiling but not really looking out; he stands at the edge of the
frame.

This makes me realize that there was in fact a death prior
to Maurice's that happened in my childhood, but that one never
counted because I only met André once, when he was already
dying, when dying was his only role. We'd flown to Paris as a

family – to see him? or was this trip already planned? – where the children, me, Mark, Katya (Kim not yet born, not yet come to our family from the orphanage in Korea) were given paper and colored pencils and settled in the small living room on a patterned rug to draw. I was very young, so young that death was still something that you did for fun and then recovered from, but we were told to draw pictures for Dédé to "cheer him up," so we did. Every now and then the colors on our paper were so exhilarating, or the strain of being still so overwhelming that we whooped aloud and someone, usually my father, would come out to hush us because death, apparently, was something that liked quiet in order to arrive.

Finally, our pictures done (the pictures to cheer Dédé up), we were told to take them to him. The room, as I recall, was darkened. The furniture was of heavy, dark wood. There was a bed with a person in it; but most vivid in my memory is my outrage that this dying man did not meet his end of the bargain, but only lay there. We'd made pictures for him. We were children. Children cheered adults. But he clearly was not interested in us or our pictures of sunny suns over smiling houses. He did not order the curtains back and the children up onto the bed to play "tent" under the sheets as we were used to doing on Saturday mornings. Saturday mornings, once my father knew he couldn't put us off any longer, he would make such tents, propping up the sheets with his long legs. But Dédé just lay there unsmiling. I don't know if Dédé died then, or later when we were gone, but I never thought much about him again.

Maurice, on the other hand, had acted delighted by us children, and so I was loyal to him. That summer before he died when I spent time in England, Kim was two and his favorite phrase was "I do dat" and this tickled Maurice. And so the memory of Maurice brings back the memory of childhood, too; it brings back me and Kim in his bowl haircut and his little blue-checked shorts with the matching button-down shirt. Each morning of that visit, Chmum let Kim toddle down the hall to fetch the milk that the milkman left by her door. Though my mother was worried that he would spill the milk and release Chmum's sharp tongue, Chmum said merely, "Be careful Kimbo;" and when he tripped one morning and the aluminum top popped off along with the plug of cream, and milk sprayed the length of the beige carpeted hall, she said only, "Don't cry, Kimbo-bim," and cleaned it up as though the milk had been delivered for that purpose.

At any rate, Uncle Maurice adopted "I do dat" for himself.

On the day he died, soon after we'd returned home from England, Chmum had a check that needed depositing. "I do dat," he said and set off to the bank where he died while standing in line.

Shortly after getting the news, I went to the bathroom. Unlike our shared bedrooms, the bathroom must have been the only truly private place in a house with four children. It had a lock and, though the tongue of the lock rattled loosely in the door-jamb whenever someone tried to get in, the door held fast. I remember sitting on the toilet and telling myself the story. "I do dat," I repeated. I saw Uncle Maurice standing in line, a big bald man slightly stooped, thinking that he was doing "dat" for Chmum. I pictured him keeling over. I thought about the other people in line, four or five of them, turning to see him on the polished floor. I thought what a shock it must be to see someone collapse like that. Although in retrospect I wonder if my grandmother told my mother this story about the bank to show her guilt that she'd let him do this errand for her, or her bitterness that life comes down to dying on the floor in a bank amongst strangers, at the time I believed it was a good story, his little gift to make us feel better.

I sat on the toilet and thought about Maurice. I wanted my eyes to get, if not full of tears, at least wet. If I could cry a little, it would mean I'd been touched by death; I wanted to be able to go to school the next day changed by the knowledge of someone's absence from the world.

But I couldn't cry. Grief, it seemed, could not be practiced. And yet, in some ways, I had practiced. I had understood that part of what makes absence acceptable is the life story that precedes it, the life story that remains. As I stood at Chmum's deathbed years later, I tried to tell her I was pregnant. By now, my mother knew; by now, I had told David he'd better hurry up and adjust. "Are you still pregnant?" he'd ask each time I called and I'd say, "Yes," impatiently; for with the deaths of my father, my brother, and soon of my grandmother, this coming baby seemed all the more necessary. I tried to tell Chmum in English. I tried in French. Finally, Chmum revived from her morphine haze, turned from the TV, grasped my hand in her hard, dry grip and said, "Ya ha! Ya ha!" – a cheer from my mother's childhood – and then something else about the dance of life.

Chmum slipped away in her sleep a few nights later, taking most of Maurice and Dédé and the rest of her dead with her, and six months after that found me driving through Berkeley with my pregnant belly swelling against the steering wheel. How right everything suddenly seemed. For the first time since the deaths in my life, I felt truly optimistic and safe. In front of me, an old woman with unruly gray hair and an armful of flapping flyers stepped into the crosswalk. I slowed and came to a stop. Thin and wrinkled and dressed in faded blue sweatpants and a bright t-shirt from Guatemala, this old woman looked just like my mother. In fact, she was my mother. I beeped the horn. My mother turned. Her face broke into a bright smile. There was something different about her. She was fully an old woman now and also younger than she'd been before her mother's death; in fact, she looked younger than she had in years. That was it. Her step was bright, her cheeks had color to them, she was smiling and waving. No longer the grieving mother, wife, and daughter, she was dancing to another tune, the tune of the expectant grandmother.

Chasm

WE TELL DR. A THAT WE NEED ANOTHER MEETING WITH him, just with him – no specialists, no residents, no social workers. It seems with him alone we can build some kind of bridge over this chasm the neurologist has opened beneath us. If Silvan will only have stiff limbs and poor grades, we would not feel suspended in quite this way. We already love him. We love him as a newborn – his loamy-scented head, the soft heft of his thighs, the tiny thump of the heart in his chest – and we love the dark-haired man with the cleft chin whom we are still in the habit of imagining he will become. But is his prognosis even compatible with future life? The neurologist has also said he may be deaf, blind, unable to move or swallow or even breathe on his own. Not only that, he's currently in a coma. He's no longer living on his own. By now, he has a fat tube down his throat to pump in air; an IV through his belly button to feed him. How long can he remain like this? How long can his life be artificially sustained?

This time Dr. A takes us to a smaller room, with a table and three chairs around it, surrounded by shelves of books. He is incredibly reasonable, patient with us. The whole time he is with us, we feel as if we are the only parents with a baby in the hospital. "This almost never happens, a baby with good prenatal care who goes through an ordinary labor," Dr. A says. He repeats what we already know: no evidence of asphyxiation on the monitor tracings, a placenta that looked fine, cord-blood gases not much below normal. These are things I am learning about. I have learned that when a baby is in distress he defecates, and that his defecation is called meconium, and that meconium is dangerous if he inhales it. I know the meconium had alerted the doctors to Silvan's distress, the meconium and his subsequent lethargy, the lethargy that had scared David so much while I lay there in my post-partum haze. But even Silvan's Apgar score – that first evaluation of a newborn's health – was not so low as that. "It still happens, more than we'd like, but less often than it used to," Dr. A concedes.

Perhaps this is said to comfort us. Or perhaps Dr. A is simply airing his own discomfort at not knowing what happened. Worldwide, I will later learn, there are four to nine million cases of birth asphyxia each year. While most babies survive it, over a million die; over a million suffer severe disability. Many of these cases are due to poverty and poor health care, but still there remain the cases that are inexplicable. In the United States, asphyxia remains the tenth leading cause of neonatal death. Many of these cases are the inexplicable kind.

Not having an explanation may be hard, but what is worse now is my suspicion of the evidence. "How can he be this damaged," I say, "when he seemed normal at birth? They took him for a few minutes, then said he was fine. Just lethargic. He even nursed." And when he nursed, I'd obeyed the nurses. I had only let him nurse a few minutes on each side, not knowing this would be the only time, not knowing he would never cry to nurse again. Perhaps I should never have stopped.

Dr. A explains. When Silvan was deprived of oxygen, the cells in his brain began to die. At first, this damage was invisible. But after cells die, they swell, and these cells are now pressing on other parts of his brain, sinking him into his coma. Because a newborn operates mostly on brain stem, and because Silvan's is still intact, he behaved before the coma, aside from the constant crying, like any newborn. His nursing was a reflex. With time, the swelling may go down, and he may return to that instinctive state. But he will still be operating only on a brain stem; he will be unable to make more than basic movements; he will never develop mentally beyond this primitive state. "If he is lucky," Dr. A explains, "he will be able to suck but not much more than that."

"But what about the neurologist yesterday? She gave us a range."

"You have to understand," Dr. A goes on in his direct and honest way, "that no prognosis is certain. Sometimes with asphyxia, there is hope. With mild cases, some children recover entirely. Or they develop mild learning and behavioral problems. But with the burst suppression pattern that we saw on the EEG ... " He tells us he stayed up much of the night researching cases of this exact pattern. "It's extremely grim," he says, shaking his head. "Extremely grim." He tries to describe the life of a child with little but a brain stem. A life of living in a hospital bed hooked up to machines. I picture a newborn in the curled-up body of an adult. I remind myself that he may not see or hear or speak or eat or move, but none of these are certain. Dr. A says he could order another test, but he suspects that this test will only confirm the grimness of the prognosis, since Silvan has already had a CAT scan and three EEGs. He wants us to know that there is a waiting list for this extra test, that it is expensive, that it would make our baby uncomfortable. He wants us to know that, despite all this, he is willing to pull rank, to insist that we go to the top of the list and have this test immediately if we need more confirmation.

With this offer, we have to make our first, concrete moral choice. Should we have another test that will make our baby uncomfortable just to make ourselves more comfortable with a prognosis that is already as certain as a prognosis can be? Should we "pull rank" over others who need this test? Should our baby receive "heroic" attention when others are dying in unnecessary, neglected misery?

I have a bag of nuts. I am ravenous post-partum. I keep the bag of nuts open between us because I must eat to keep up my strength for these conversations in which so much must be heard and acted on. My appetite is endless. I offer Dr. A some nuts. He takes one politely, allowing me to mother him because he is compassionate and maybe understands that the need to mother someone is raging in me.

"So the range was to give us hope?" David asks.

"A prognosis is never certain."

"We understand that," David says. "But if the prognosis is as grim as it sounds, we need to know what this means for his life."

Dr. A begins with telling us that Silvan may never revive from the coma, or he may die of a seizure. Or, if he does revive and try to nurse, lack of coordination will cause him to inhale milk each time. This inhalation of food will give him recurrent pneumonia. He will have to return to the hospital over and over to be saved. He will most likely die before reaching the age of one, but he may go on longer than that.

"What would have happened if he hadn't been given oxygen at birth?" I suddenly ask. After all, this was why they had wheeled him away, to revive him. And right before this meeting, a nurse let slip that Silvan had started turning blue again that very morning. This is why he is now on a breathing tube. "You should have seen us running around to save him," she said. I am starting to understand that already many choices have been made about his life without my knowledge.

"That's hard to know for sure," Dr. A says, "but unlike adults who struggle to breathe, babies react to a deficit of oxygen by breathing less and less until they stop breathing altogether. He may have just slipped away."

"How frustrating," I say.

"How so?"

"To think that we are in this situation because he was saved."

"We couldn't let him die at birth," Dr. A says. "Not before we knew what was wrong with him."

"Of course not," I say, but still I am frustrated. He has been stopped from dying in the most peaceful way possible. He's been thwarted in the only act he's tried to take.

"But what if we think it's wrong now to keep saving him?" David asks.

"Some parents don't treat the pneumonia. They allow their children to die that way."

"And some parents let them die of seizures?" I ask.

"It happens sometimes."

"How awful," I say. "Is there no other way to let him die?"

And so, he tells us. He tells us that in the case of a newborn with a prognosis as grim as Silvan's, coupled with a coma and inability to take nourishment orally, it is legal to withdraw all food and liquid. I have no memory of this moment, the shock of learning this truth that, though euthanasia is illegal, you can starve a person to death. I do not remember the sound of Dr. A's voice, nor his actual words. What I remember instead is that one moment I am in despair for Silvan, and the next I have hope.

CEASING TO EAT used to be the most common precursor to death, prior to feeding tubes and other interventions, prior to medical situations such as ours. Most deaths prior to the twentieth century were preceded by a few weeks of illness, then a few days of not eating. People used to recognize the approach of death this way, the body's natural way of letting go. Instead of being painful, it seems that giving up food has a palliative effect. This effect doesn't happen for people who are trying not to starve, children who are getting tiny amounts of food or liquid, for example. But within twenty-four hours of giving up all nourishment, our bodies enter a state in which appetite is suppressed, pain diminishes and we feel euphoric. This is what happens when people fast. We can't know for sure, but this seems also to be the case for people who are dying.

This is what Dr. A tells us, after we ask. For of course I don't want Silvan to suffer more in dying than he would in living. I need to know what he is in for. However, Dr. A warns us, "Newborns are born with great reserves of fat. With a healthy newborn, this can take a long time."

"How long?" David asks.

Dr. A doesn't know for sure. "It could be weeks. If you decide to go this route, we'll make sure he's comfortable of course. We'll have morphine, and also lube for his eyes and lips if they get dry."

As if to test Dr. A's confidence, David asks, "What would you do in this situation if it were your child?" But Dr. A only smiles sadly, shakes his head. "You are the parents. You have to decide. I know it's hard..." And then, "I was once in a situation like this, almost in a situation like this, with my wife." Though Dr. A has not told us how he himself would act, it is comforting to know that he has at least *imagined* himself in our situation, that it is possible to imagine such a death.

Dr. A wants us to go home and think about our decision before taking any action, but how strangely certain I feel. If Silvan should be spared his life, there seems no justification for stalling. I feel as if I have been studying for this moment my whole life. Now is when I will pass or fail. I can't ask Silvan what he would want for himself, so I have to rely on what I would want for myself, what I believe about life and death, what makes it good or bad. For now, this knowledge is purely instinctual. If I love him, I will let him go.

Dr. A looks exhausted from being doctor to a child he cannot cure but remains patient and present. He declines eating more of my nuts but does not stir from his chair.

"Are you sure?" he asks over and over.

Silvan may die at any time but he might not and we need a plan, a plan to make up for the fact that his life has been artificially saved until now. We will start by removing the phenobarbital, we decide. "Without the phenobarbital, Silvan may wake up. Or he may have a seizure and die," Dr. A warns us and waits to see how we react. We nod. "If he doesn't die of a seizure, we can remove his breathing tube. Again, he may die; or he may not." Again, we nod. "If he keeps breathing, we can remove the intravenous food." At each step, we nod.

"Are you sure?" he repeats.

Suddenly I have a question. "Will the nurses..." I say. Just as suddenly, my voice breaks. Dr. A looks alarmed. Have I become unsure after all these hours? "Will the nurses be kind... to a baby...who is dying?"

Panforte

PERHAPS CRISIS ALWAYS BRINGS US BACK TO CHILDHOOD, but I seem to be reverting. As we prepare to leave the hospital that night – Dr. A still wants us to go home and think about our decision before taking any action – we run into an acquaintance. She works on a different floor but has heard about Silvan through mutual friends. She has been looking for us to tell me what she tells very few people – she had a stillbirth before she went on to have the rest of her children. She is very beautiful, with smooth, olive skin and green eyes that mock the dull green of her scrubs. Her living children, whom I have met at a party, are just as beautiful. Standing too close to me, her earnest eyes on my face, she says, "I want you to know that whatever happens, you are strong enough to survive this."

And I resist her comfort. "You were probably *younger* than me when you lost your first," I say, as if my suffering needs to be greater than hers, as if this is a competition I need to win to make what I am losing acceptable, as if by proving that I am the champion of pain, I will be rewarded enough to make this pain worthwhile.

"But I had fertility issues," this well-meaning friend of a friend says, opening her green eyes wider, playing along. We take a step away from each other, squaring off like fighters.

"Of course," I say, catching myself, "you're right. Thank you."

IT ISN'T FAIR, I think bitterly on the way home in the car; and then I remember my father trying to teach me not to think this way. "Nothing's fair in life," was his constant refrain, his greatest moral teaching, used mostly to head off petty arguments. Thursday evenings in my childhood, my father always had to "hold down the fort" as he put it, while my mother had choir practice down at the church. One Thursday evening in particular, my perfumed mother came wafting through the dining room, kissing us all goodnight, leaving my father in charge of a special dessert. There it sat, a *panforte* smaller than a Frisbee and many times heavier, all blackened fruit and nuts, on a plate beside him. I couldn't believe our luck–*panforte* on this ordinary Thursday night–it felt like Christmas. He began the task of cutting and distributing as equally as he could to four kids. He passed the first piece to me. Then I watched him cut the next. It was a good-looking piece, too, and as I would relate it to myself later, I thought, *I will be polite and pass this down to Katya.*

Abruptly, my father changed the position of his knife. "For holding out for a bigger piece than your sister," he said, "you get half."

I howled at the injustice. I told him I was being polite, generous, self-sacrificing. When he didn't believe me, I stormed from the room to hide beneath my green desk, pulling the desk chair in after me. From the comfort of my little green cage, I told myself I was right. By refusing to come out, I was punishing my father. When he saw the unfairness of my suffering, my father would give me the respect I deserved. But the longer I sat, the more complex things became. Even as I stewed in righteous pride, I felt as if my father could see a deeper truth. He could read between the lines of my own story. For the truth was, had that next piece not looked equal to the one in front of me, I would not have passed mine down whereas my father wanted me to accept that, even if the next piece was smaller, my life was fine. He wanted me to be grateful for *whatever* I got–and I refused. For being good, for caring about others, for suffering enough myself on behalf of those others, I thought I deserved at least the same as everybody else.

"IT'S NOT FAIR," I say to David anyway when we get home that night. The certainty of our beautiful green-eyed acquaintance that I will survive has not comforted me, coming from someone who has reached the other side. *A stillbirth is easier*, I think cruelly; *she went on to have more children; she has no idea what I am suffering.* Instead of letting myself be crushed by what we're enduring, I swell with arrogance over it.

But David is like my father. He won't brook melodrama. "If anything," he says, "we're lucky Silvan's prognosis is as bad as it is." And that's true. Although Dr. A has said David and I need to discuss this further, we barely need words to come to agreement. Because Silvan's prognosis is as bad as it is, because something much worse than stiff limbs and poor grades are in his future, we aren't faced with as much of a moral quandary, as much of a threat to our marriage. Silvan is in a coma. He's being kept alive artificially. Even if he revives, he'll never be able to survive on his own. Even if he revives, it will be to a life of constant dying. We sit on the couch together holding hands and feeling certain. We are still in shock; in some part of ourselves, we must still believe the baby we're waiting for has not yet arrived. But at the same time, we're certain this very same baby has arrived and is ready now to leave. We need such certainty to act.

"We have to tell Dr. A tomorrow that we're ready," I say.

David gets up to call his father and stepmother, his mother, his sister. In addition to talking about it with each other, Dr. A has said we need to find out how our family members feel before taking any action. I lie on the couch listening to David on the phone, explaining. When he gets off, he tells me everyone is in agreement it's for the best. He says they sounded relieved that a decision has been made. David's mother had to make a similar choice for her own mother a few years before. Awful as it is, we are in intellectual agreement.

My family, I know, will also be in intellectual agreement, but still I hesitate to tell them. My mother especially. I hesitate even though I know she was there for all those family dinner table conversations in the 1970s when Karen Ann Quinlan was lying in her coma. All through my grammar and high school years, Quinlan appeared in the paper, her sober smile and smooth brown hair parted in the middle, Quinlan held up as a reason not to get carried away at parties. Thanks to this girl whose parents fought for the right to remove her from a ventilator, I have been able to make this choice for Silvan. Thanks to her, I know that my mother also does not believe in pushing life beyond reason. My mother has even given me a copy of her own living will and granted me power of attorney and had me store these documents in case I need them in a similar situation for her someday. Still, I hesitate because I dread her suffering. "Pretend that you are Christian children," my mother used to say in despair at our unwillingness to sacrifice, to suffer for our siblings. Her refrain was more confusing than my father's line about nothing being fair in life – for we *were* Christian children; no matter how much we sinned, we had been *baptized*. But I know that somehow she equates suffering with love, and through her own suffering she hopes to carry ours.

In fact, her suffering for Silvan began before he was even born, when he was barely visible as a swelling of my belly. There we were on her deck having lunch – egg salad sandwiches and cucumber salad – and she was arguing with David about the baby. Though she had loved our wedding ceremony, though she'd found so many things that the renewal rabbi said reminiscent of Christianity, she was shocked that our baby would not be baptized; she even had a baptismal gown ready. Why did David's Jewish background "trump" my Catholic? When David pointed out that it was possible to be a non-practicing Jewish atheist but not a Catholic one, that baptism is religious, not cultural, she said, "But what if the baby *dies* and ends up in limbo?"

"Maureen," David asked, "why would the baby die?"

"Babies *do* still die, you know," she said

"But the chances of that happening…"

"And what about David," I broke in. "Do you think David will go to hell?

"Oh, no," my mother said, shocked, "because David's such a sweetheart."

I want to call and remind her of this. I want to say that Silvan is a sweetheart. That he will go to heaven whether he is baptized or not. I remember how I used to add, as a child, the addendum to every prayer "…or whatever You think is best." In this way, I'd tried to preserve my faith from the shock of not always getting what I wanted. Does she not know such tricks? She must be wondering how God can do this to us after all we have lost as a family. She must be hoping that through her own suffering she will be able to lessen my own. "It's not fair," I say out loud. It feels so good to revert that I say it again, shouting into the sofa cushions, "It's not fair, it's not fair, it's not fair."

A Choice

THE NEXT DAY FINDS US ALL TOGETHER IN THE HALLWAY, my mother, my brother Kim, David, and me. It seems as if my sister Katya must be there as well, but she is still far away in Brazil. Only five days have passed since Silvan's birth, but it feels much longer. So then it is the four of us in a knot in the hall. I need to tell them. It's a peculiar position, and yet not as uncommon in the modern era as one might think. Medicine, which used to be the practice of keeping people alive long enough for nature to heal them, became in the twentieth century a success story. Medicine can now cure people. And in the twenty-first century, medicine has progressed to a point that most people in the United States no longer die of a disease. Instead, most people die of a *choice* to stop treating whatever diseases they have. Difficult as it is to choose death, every day people have to choose – for themselves, for parents, spouses, siblings, and even for children.

So we stand there in the way of other parents going to scrub their hands free of germs, in the way of nurses and doctors, in the way of gurneys with babies on them being pushed from one room to another, feeling wrong. For though people are making this choice every day, hope is still what we expect from medicine, and choosing death seems a failure. So we stand awkwardly, trying to begin. Just then the social worker appears at my side. Ever since we met for the first time in the Bad News Room, she has seemed strangely ineffective, hesitant, like a passing stranger sucked unwillingly into someone else's drama

on her day off. "Couple treats each other tenderly," she has
written in her notes, so we know she's watching us, making sure
we're equipped to deal, but we're unsure how equipped she is
herself. "Is there anything I can do to help?" she says now, looking scared because when we decline her help, as we always do,
she will be at a loss.

But this time there's something concrete she can do. We
need somewhere to talk. Without her. Perhaps in the privacy
of her office. She hesitates, then decides she can do this. We file
in, settle in a circle. She leaves, closing the door behind her.
Alone together, I tell them, "We have decided to remove Silvan
from all life support: oxygen, food, liquid." Everyone looks grim,
gray, shocked, as if we ourselves are the ones receiving the
death sentence.

David tries to explain the diagnosis and prognosis. Even
if Silvan survives his coma, he will be damaged beyond what
they've ever seen, bedridden day and night, unable to control
his limbs, his saliva, his mind. He might grow to look as if he
has an inner life in the way he writhes and moans, but the brain
scans suggest he won't actually have a life beyond his brain
stem. I explain that, if we kept him alive now in the misplaced
hope that somehow he might regain more of his brain function,
we'd have to cross this bridge over and over each time his body
tried to die. Kim is nodding and fighting tears. He will tell me
later how the shock of this loss seemed to enter him and join to
all his other losses and begin to shake him to pieces.

But my mother doesn't seem really to have heard us yet.

In addition to the distant look in her eyes, my mother is
wearing a windbreaker so worn, so scudded with white, so
threadbare and diaphanous, that its original color is a mystery.
In clothing such as this, she was mistaken once at her church
for a homeless woman instead of a volunteer come to help the
homeless. She still dresses well to teach, but she is slowly
retiring, and every few months it seems, she threatens to leave
us all for the nunnery where she can do "more good" praying

for the world than she can by living an ordinary life amongst us. How she suffers on behalf of others. How generous and not materialistic. How strong she has always been, raising four children, foster parenting, teaching full time, nursing the ill, grieving the dead, not at all afraid of death for herself; and how weak as well for not being able to bear the pain of others – as if it is her job to bear it for us. What is she thinking now with her eyes on the middle distance? Is she praying for some sort of miracle? What miracle would that be?

YEARS LATER, MY mother will explain. "No one was helpful to me. Everyone had a story for me, but they were all stories of hope," and she will give me a few examples from letters sent by friends: "He was not expected to live, but now he's a strapping young man going off to Oxford…" or "Caretakers come to learn something from such damaged children and feel that they are here for a reason…" Years later, she will say she still sometimes wonders if she could've prayed hard enough for a miracle.

My mother is at a loss. With no one to talk to her about accepting the death that she has been worrying about since before Silvan was born, she doesn't know how to talk to me about it. I know she will accept my choice. My mother, for all her suffering, is entirely supportive. It is not that she is meek or over-indulgent. She certainly speaks her mind. It is only that she knows where the line is between loving and controlling her children. Perhaps she only wants to make sure I am solid in my choice. Perhaps she wants to make sure David and I have considered more than one opinion, just as she has, allowing herself to be buffeted by opinions, trusting that only out of confusion can a solid choice come. As her eyes return to the room, she begins to pepper us with questions.

"How do you know the prognosis is right?" she asks first.

We tell her we can't know for sure, but for us to gamble otherwise seems unfair to Silvan.

"And what if someone else were willing to care for him?"

"Like you?"

"Like me," she says, "though I don't how long I'll still be alive."

"If I thought he should be kept alive, I would do it. He's my son."

"Of course he is," she says.

"If Daddy were here," I say, "he would agree with this choice." Kim and my mother both looked startled by this entry of the dead, but it feels just right to me. Here comes my father, deep with feeling but strong and calm. If only he were here, he and my mother could go home together and talk this out together. Instead, I explain on his behalf. "You and Daddy always said you'd never want to live as vegetables." Kim looks surprised. I suppose that, being ten years younger than me, by the time he was ready for adult conversation at the dinner table, the topic was no longer Karen Ann Quinlan and the line between life and death; or the conversations he remembers are the ones that have been useful to him as an adult. As with all siblings, our stories of growing up in the same family are different. Or perhaps it's simpler than that. Perhaps additional dead family is more than he can handle right now.

"But that was *us*," my mother says now. "*We* wouldn't want to live that way."

"So why should Silvan have to?"

She looks abashed.

"You could even say God called him and we are preventing him from going," I say. "After all, he was revived after birth. Maybe that was playing God when God really wanted him to die then. In fact, he's been revived several times. He keeps trying to die and we're preventing him."

"You could say that," she says, but she still looks worried. She chews her nails so loudly I can hear it across the room. I say, "Stop chewing your nails," and she looks up startled, then laughs. She takes her duty to do good very seriously but she does not take herself too seriously. David thinks this means she will eventually laugh at her own "neurosis" about Silvan's soul, but I don't. I know that if she can't save Silvan's life with prayer, she will at least want to save his soul.

Confirmation

THAT AFTERNOON, I CALL FATHER B FROM HOME WHILE
David stays at the hospital with Silvan. What we are doing for
Silvan feels compassionate, what we are doing is not euthanasia,
but I wonder if my mother feels the distinction. This is important
because I know the Catholic Church agrees with the government: it is against euthanasia. I know this with all the visceral
weight of discovering it on my own, one foggy afternoon in
San Francisco when I was in high school. For some reason, I had
chosen euthanasia as my topic for a school report. Because of
Karen Ann Quinlan and those dinner table conversations, I knew
there was controversy about what Quinlan's parents had done. I
thought what they had done was euthanasia. I assumed this
meant the church was for it and the legal system against it and I
was feeling righteous about the church's loving stance. Certain
of my case, I set out after school for the Catholic bookstore to research my topic. A middle-aged woman in a gray cardigan helped
me to a slim pamphlet, and back out on the street, I caught
my bus where the only thing I gleaned from the dense pages was
the Church's condemnation of what I'd thought they would
champion. I sat there in my itchy, wool school uniform in shock.
The church was against what I thought of as linked with only
positives: compassion, acceptance of the inevitability of death.
In my dictionary, the first definition seemed to agree. "An easy
death," the dictionary said, as if anyone could argue against that.

I soon had a chance to argue the issue beyond the abstract,

to experience its true complexity. A girl in the youth group I attended Sunday nights at my church had an accident and fell into an irreversible coma and her parents chose to remove her from life support. At the end of the week, the breathing tube would be removed. The novitiates who ran the youth group presented this as a reasonable and loving option, a Catholic option, and this confused me. Hadn't I just done a school report in which I had to say that the church was against euthanasia? I still hadn't understood the distinction between euthanasia and allowing someone to die. Even more confusing was the fact that until this day, I'd never liked this girl. Kirsten had swishy blond hair, giggled constantly, and attracted every boy in the room while never once looking at me. But hearing she might die, I wondered if God were testing me. Perhaps Quinlan's parents had been wrong after all, perhaps Kirsten's parents were wrong. Perhaps the church was wrong. Perhaps they had all lost faith in the miracles of saints.

The week Kirsten was in her coma I struggled towards the peak of my religious faith. I wondered if this was God calling me at last. Each night in bed, I ran through my fantasy: running past hospital security, reaching Kirsten's bed, putting my healing hands on her. But always I felt the same discomfort when she opened her eyes. If I didn't even like her, how could I hope to heal her better than the parents who loved her? At last the day came, life support was removed, Kirsten died. That night, we gathered in youth group with unusual solemnity. Kirsten's peals of laughter were absent. We gathered in a great circle with the lights off and passed a candle from hand to hand. In that golden silence, we could hear each other breathing and I understood. The call I'd felt was not the call of God after all. It had been the call of guilt, the call of vanity, whereas here in this room was real love. Kirsten's parents had made this choice because they loved her. And as I had this humble thought, the candle reached me and something beautiful happened. I felt Kirsten's soul and my soul joining and rising up towards God together.

Thinking to preserve this heady sense of souls in union, I

wrote to the Bishop of Oakland and asked to be confirmed early into the Church. I was fifteen and didn't want to have to wait until his next visit to our parish two years later. I'd felt God's presence, I told him in my letter. But the Bishop was busy. He wasn't impressed with my plea. And two years later, as I lay on the rug in a little room off the sacristy during confirmation class listening to an old priest drone on about the Holy Spirit, it occurred to me that this beautiful thing – this Jiminy-Cricket-like conscience that would sit on my shoulder as a stand-in for God, part of his mysterious trinity, to help me choose right from wrong – was something only a priest could confer through the sacrament of confirmation, and I didn't like that fact. "That's right," the priest said when I asked him to confirm this. Dignified and silly, the priest rocked back and forth on his heels, hands resting on the round belly beneath his cassock, and he seemed too ordinary an intermediary between me and the transcendent love I yearned for.

Father B, on the other hand, is a priest I like. Father B is smart, reasonable, kind. He is no longer a priest at our parish – I'm no longer a member of any parish – but he has a long history with our family. He came up to the house when Mark died, he conducted the "laying on of the hands" when my father was first ill, he blessed our wedding rings. Even David likes Father B. My mother thinks that if Father B had conducted my confirmation class, I'd still be a member of the church. I don't know if this is true, but I do know that removing life support is an uncomfortable act, and I sense Father B will be able to speak about it to my mother in a way that is supportive. Mostly, I want him to talk to her about heaven. After all, my mother has turned in torment to Father B with questions about Mark's soul. People who commit suicide are guilty, the church believes, of a sin as grave as murder, punishable by hell; our modern understanding of mental illness has only just begun to soften that condemnation. And yet Father B has told my mother that Mark is in heaven. If Father B has said this about Mark, surely he must believe that an unbaptised baby will go there as well. Despite Saint Augustine's condemnation of such babies to limbo, the church must generally be softening in favor of a heaven more comforting to grieving parents. But Father B surprises me. When I tell him I am calling on behalf of my mother, he says, "Do I sense that a part of you is worried about Silvan's soul, too?"

"IS THERE?" DAVID asks me now. I am back at the hospital and we are standing over Silvan's little bed together. Our hands run over his body as if our constant touch is as necessary to keep him here as his blood's circulation, or his breath. I have just told David about my conversation with Father B. "Is a part of you worried about his soul?"

"Oh, no," I say, "If there's a heaven, all souls go." I don't know if I believe in heaven anymore, let alone souls; and as I say it, I realize I have not even prayed for Silvan yet. What happened to my need for prayer? When I was young, I used to pray for everything. When Mark was ill, I prayed. When my father was ill, I prayed. But after that? After all those prayers went unanswered? I am here with Silvan, standing over his bed, simply trying to accept that he too will die, and that life will go on without him.

"So what did you tell Father B?"

"I told him I'm worried about my mother."

David nods. "And what did Father B say?"

"He said he can tell my mother what he tells lots of grandparents in this situation. She can baptize Silvan herself, just with water, or even by desire alone, that she doesn't even have to tell us."

I feel such relief, but David is horrified. "Silvan's Jewish."

"But if you don't even believe in baptism," I say, "who cares? It's just a little water." I can even picture the water, in a little plastic bottle from the trip to Lourdes when I was young, saved in a back corner of the kitchen cabinet all these years. Though nothing in me needs Silvan baptized, it's easy for me to imagine how much someone might still need to believe. This is my mother's way of caring.

"But why do it if it's just water? What does it matter?" he asks.

"It matters to *her*."

"But it's so illogical, it's so obviously made up," David says.

"But if it's made up," I say, "why do you even care? "

SHORTLY AFTER THIS conversation, Sister C shows up at Silvan's bedside. Now it's David who has gone home, to return the messages building up on our answering machine; and I am alone with Silvan. He's wearing only a diaper under his heat lamp, and I admire the frog-like spread of his chubby legs, the crow's-foot of wrinkles raying out from his armpit, the little starfish hand that I hold in mine. Though Sister C is the "non-denominational" chaplain for the hospital and wears lay clothes, she is obviously a Catholic nun. Exhausted perhaps from all these conversations, from this struggle between my mother and my husband about something that matters so little to me, my first response to her is to echo David. "My son is *Jewish*." I'm startled by my own vehemence. What does this even mean for a comatose newborn? Perhaps I'm afraid that she will try to interfere with our decision; that she will appeal to the side of me that once yearned for sainthood; remind me of my namesake Saint Monica who spent her life praying for the soul of her sinful son Augustine; make me feel bad about my soul and the soul of my own son. Or perhaps I'm just being loyal to my husband. I keep hold of Silvan's hand.

Sister C smiles. "So he's Jewish. I'm still wondering if there's anything I can do for you or for him."

With her question, I understand why she's here. She's here to relieve suffering. And so I beg her, gesturing with my free hand, "Take care of my mother. She's Catholic like you. She's out in the hall saying her rosary. She wants to baptize him."

Already I am turning away with relief.

"Is that all?" Sister C asks. "Nothing for you?"

But I have returned to Silvan, to his little body, here and now.

Distillation

FOR NOW, SILVAN LIES ASLEEP AS USUAL, THREADED with tubes and wires and the medical tape that holds it all in place. He is five days old, and nothing has changed. We have a plan, but Dr. A still wants us to wait, as if we ourselves might change. Silvan has not opened his eyes since his first night of life; a fat tube in the mouth helps him breathe; thin tubes give him fluids and medicine. To help us hold him, nurses transfer him with all his equipment onto a pillow, and then pass the pillow to us. For all of this, Silvan seems sweetly asleep. He has the flushed cheeks and lips of a baby who has just finished nursing. He keeps his two little fists curled up, one on either side of his face, the way I do sometimes in bed because I find it comforting. I watch him lying calmly on a pillow in my brother Kim's lap.

Now at last when we have made our decision, there is time just to mother Silvan.

At the next bed, a mother and grandmother of a baby who is ready to go home sit silent as always, taking turns feeding and burping their baby. They seem self-conscious about speaking to him in the silly way that people usually speak to babies. The only words they speak are to each other. Perhaps they will be less self-conscious once they get him home alone but I doubt it. Although they were told weeks before that he was ready, the mother is afraid. Afraid that he will choke on his food at home and die. Perhaps he is brain damaged too. I smile at them and turn to my baby who will never go home.

With Silvan on Kim's lap, I find I can reach his little face through his equipment more easily than I can when he's on my own. I bend to kiss his forehead, then his nose, then the space by his ear that is free of medical tape. And then I cannot stop. I kiss the front of his neck below the breathing tube, those warm wrinkles, and the side of his neck, so smooth, so smooth, and his shoulder, and the creases at the edge of his armpit and across his naked sternum and down towards his belly button, all the while making smacking noises, eating him up.

When I raise my head I am renewed as if, after hours on the trail, I have found water. But Kim is inscrutable. A distant smile on his face. I think of the kisses I gave *him*, kisses just like these, when he was a baby newly arrived from Korea. I think of his birth mother, too, wondering if she kissed him like this, the newborn she was about to let go. If so, I feel linked to her pain.

The mother and grandmother at the next crib stare in surprise.

"That was quite a kiss," the grandmother says.

"Well, once I started I couldn't stop," I say.

My time is limited. This is a mother's love distilled.

"SOME PARENTS TAKE weeks and weeks to make this decision," Nurse Kerry says in praise, standing with us in the door to his little room. Nothing has changed. Or rather, we have stopped the flow of phenobarbital and Silvan has carried on. We'd thought he might die of a seizure; now we are relieved that he has not.

Nurse Kerry is a new nurse, very young, and this is her first terminal baby; she is sweetly emotional, her fresh young skin flushes pink and her big eyes gleam with tears as she talks. Dr. A has secured this tiny private room for us so that we don't have to suffer the extremity of our grief in the middle of the nursery floor. "And don't forget," she says, "there's always morphine to make this easier."

For a moment, I think she is speaking in code. I think: *At last, here is someone who will help him die more easily*. For I am still in shock that not feeding him is an option. I'm hoping we don't have to go that far. I'm hoping nature will be merciful. Whatever she reads on my face, she blushes, says, "I mean, to make him comfortable."

EVEN IN HIS coma, Silvan seems uncomfortable. He has begun tugging with a hand at his breathing tube. Some babies have been known to "extubate" themselves this way. Seeing that little hand tug, I'm frantic and aching to give him this simple relief, even if it means he will die, right then and there, in my lap.

I arrive in the morning prepared. Silvan is six days old.

But it turns out that sometime in the night, our private room has been given away to a contagious baby. Now they're cleaning the room to give back to Silvan before they extubate him. I'm frantic to be with him, to relieve him, to know if he will die or live. But we're stuck outside in the hallway. My mother is pacing with her rosary and Sister C when my nerves are at their frazzled worst. If Silvan has been baptized by now, I don't ask. Instead, I swear in front of Sister C – "They're taking so goddamned long to clean the room," I say, before clapping my hand over my mouth – but Sister C is, of course, unfazed by my swearing and eager to help. She rushes off to see if she can speed the process.

At last the room is ready. I sit in the rocking chair. Someone transfers Silvan to my lap. Gently, gently, Nurse Kerry peels away the tape that's been holding the tube in place for almost a week. Dr. A begins to pull the long tube out. It's unbearably long. I cannot look. But at last, he is free and there he is, my little Silvan. Just like that, he closes his mouth. He lifts his little hands up towards his face. One hand settles under his chin, the other cups his tape-reddened cheek. He breathes.

He breathes and seems to smile.

NOW EVERYONE POURS in to see him. In our private room, there seems no limit to the number of visitors; we are bending all the rules. We photograph him free of his breathing tube, we photograph him in the arms of grandparents, uncles, aunts, friends.

Free of the tube, he is also free to lie on his stomach. Noticing his backside is red, I try to put him down on his stomach for the night. When a nurse comes in and says she isn't comfortable with that, I ask, "Why not? Are you afraid he'll stop breathing?" but I return him to his back.

Desperate for him to stop breathing, I am in love with every breath he takes.

NINE DAYS FROM birth we say that we are ready. The anticipation is awful. That morning, I can barely leave the house. In the same way that I was both inside and outside myself when I heard of his brain damage, my grief is both overwhelming and melodramatic. I'm on all fours in the living room heaving, gasping for breath at the thought of becoming a mother who is not feeding her child. David holds me from behind, trying to get me to stop; then I am no longer crying from the depths, I'm coming back up to the surface where I am sure of what we have to do.

Back at the hospital, I'm stunned by how much more exquisite he is in the flesh than in any image I can hold in my mind. His skin calls to me to stroke it. His head must be sniffed. When he pees, I marvel. I can't help being proud. Of his long bones. Of his long eyelashes. We say that we are ready.

Hours later, I notice a bag of fluid still hanging from his IV pole.

I call a nurse in and ask, "Why is he still getting food?"

She looks upset. She says, "I'm just letting that last bag run out."

"Okay," I say to her. *Okay*, I say to myself.

Let him die easily, I think at each step; and then again, not yet.

We Climb

WHATEVER LUCIDITY, WHATEVER STRENGTH I HAVE IS partly biological. My body is healing apace: my stitches are healing, my womb shrinking, my milk drying up. Not only that, crisis releases hormones that make our brains and bodies work faster, more efficiently, our senses sharpen, we become less sensitive to pain, our memories work better. As if this is normal, as if we have lived a lifetime together like this – David, Silvan, and me – we adjust to crisis.

Sleep, spend day at hospital, sleep.

Each day stretches long as a year.

A lifetime is packed into a week.

One night, I notice the chill of almost-summer fog coming in from the ocean, on another I register that the month is now May, but none of this means time is really passing. Not the way it used to. Things are happening in the world, bad things, other children suffering in the headlines without medical care in war-torn countries while my son dies surrounded by equipment; I know this is unfair, but there is hardly room for other people yet. I'm still waiting for the end of his first day. But with his healthy heart and lungs, his great reserves of fat, no one knows how long he will go on. If anything feels miraculous to us, it is this ability to go on. Sometimes I can't believe he's not still inside of me. "I have a son," I record in my diary as if to make it true.

In addition to starting a diary, I let myself sleep in. I wake from tortured dreams. No longer pregnant, I dream about

having been pregnant and giving birth to a baby who's not okay.
I wake from the dream relieved, until I realize it's true. I fall
asleep and have another dream. Silvan is saying, "Linda, Linda,"
which is the name of his paternal grandmother who has yet
to meet him. I'm desperate to find the neurologist to see if this
changes the prognosis. Is it too late to reverse the effects of not
feeding him?

"I have a son who is dying," I write in my diary. "I have a
son whom I have chosen to let die." My mind is trying to understand, my mind is searching for patterns.

During the day, I feel ready. I say it out loud: "I'm ready.
I love you. You can go." But at night, my tune changes. "Don't go,"
I say, leaning over his crib, "until I'm back in the morning" as if
he will understand my words and do all he can to make this easy
for me.

If I have faith, if I have hope, it is not that a god will over-
hear and grant me this wish. It is rather that between us we
have some power to do this right, to pay close enough attention
that we can let go when we both are ready. I am thinking of my
friend Maggy Brown and her mother. I'm thinking of the tender
certainty of youth. This was the first Sunday in college, the first
delicious day of deciding not to go to church, and Maggy had
invited me to spend the day studying with her. Though Maggy
seemed so much wilder than me, with her crazy black hair,
her boasts of debauchery, she seemed familiar too. She'd come
from a big Catholic family in Wisconsin; she liked to drink wine.
I accepted her invitation, and we set out from our dorm to find the
perfect spot. We found it at the edge of campus, a slope of lush,
forgotten grass overflowing into a nature preserve full of spindly,
leaning trees. We lay in the dappled shade with our books spread
before us and pretended to read about the death of Achilles.
Overhead, white clouds swelled. All around us, bees hummed,
alighting on the clover flowers, on our books, on our hands and
hair as we blossomed.

"My mother was dying of breast cancer my whole child-hood," Maggy explained to me then, "that's why I was sent away to a boarding school for wild youth." So here was someone who'd actually survived my greatest fear, and I listened intently. "She sent for me at school so she could say goodbye, and then she held out until Easter."

How moved I was. Though Maggy said she no longer believed in God herself, she believed her mother believed and that, because of this faith, she was able to die when everyone was ready. This was a faith I could embrace, a belief in the power of belief. I told her that I too had lost my faith but I wanted to believe in something greater than ourselves that linked us.

I found a four-leaf clover then; Maggy found a four-leaf clover; there were lots of four-leaved clovers suddenly, and we made wishes on them.

We were young and we were going to survive the dying all around us.

"You're the first person," Maggy said, "I've ever met who can talk about death. You can deal."

I shrugged, hiding my pleasure.

FOR MOST OF the morning as I resist rushing straight back to the hospital, we are occupied by the ringing of the phone. Family calls every morning in order, my mother, David's father, David's sister. Later in the day, his mother, his stepmother, sometimes my brother. In between, we get calls from the hospital, from outside specialists, from friends. People call from all over the world – how fortunate we feel – Washington D.C., Oregon, even Israel. One friend calls every morning at ten a.m. from New Mexico. The calls are brief but crucial. She lets me do the talking. Her husband has told her he no longer loves her after twenty-one years to-gether and is going to leave her and their newborn baby, but she doesn't tell me this. For now, she considers the bigger crisis to be mine. She says she just wants to make sure that I get out of bed.

For my doula, I don't get out of bed. Her messages sound

angry and impatient. Studies show the consistent, calm presence of another woman can help ease labor, which is why we'd hired a doula, but now she wants to know what the hospital did wrong and when we will have an answer. She doesn't sound like she should be in the business of birthing children; she sounds too impatient, too shocked that something has gone wrong. Even while I was in labor, I realize, she sounded wrong, more concerned about her own comfort than mine, complaining about her lack of sleep, her hunger. I try not to think about her and us together in that distant time.

On the other hand, for my obstetrician, I run to the phone. Because she was not the one to deliver him, because he was born on the one day she'd warned me she could not come, I can still be loyal to her. That first week, when she comes to the hospital to meet Silvan, I like how she says, "Oh my," taking Silvan from my arms, "everyone told me how beautiful he was, and I thought, *yeah, yeah, I've seen newborns before ...*" I like the way she has to pause to control her voice, "but he really is exquisite, isn't he?" I like her present too – she's the only person to have brought a present – an angel bear with wings and halo that David hangs above Silvan's crib. I like the honesty of her present.

While she is visiting, she checks my leg. Though I have been trying to take care of myself, to eat and sleep, I sit hunched over Silvan for so long that my feet and legs are swollen and now I have a cramp so severe in my calf that it is hard to walk. Worried that maybe it was a blood clot that damaged Silvan, and that I might be prone to them myself, she sends me to a specialist when the cramp won't go away.

On the day I go, the waiting room is full of old people who look as if they've been waiting there for years, but I am rushed right in. This new doctor hooks me up to a machine. He shows me on a monitor how my valves open and shut to let blood flow through my leg like sand through an hourglass. He praises my venous valves. "There's nothing wrong with your leg," he says. "Let me get you back to your baby." I am grateful but also strangely bitter to hear that my body goes on healthily as if indifferent to whatever injured Silvan.

AFTER THE SCARE with my leg, David insists that we not only eat and sleep well, but that we spend more time away from the hospital moving our bodies while other people stay behind to hold Silvan. One day, we go down to the park at the Berkeley marina. It's an unusual, still, slightly-muggy afternoon. No one is there. We go a different route than usual, away from the water and into a hollow between hills. I am still walking slowly, still swollen and loose from giving birth, so we don't plan to go far. Wildflowers riot on the hillsides. We go to see up close. There is an old man there, with wild hair and billowing clothes and four dogs roaming around him. He keeps leering at me. David wants to use the Porta-Potty but is nervous leaving me with the man. We climb up to the wildflowers and then David makes a dash to the Porta-Potty as the man calls his dogs to leave. As the man wanders off, he looks over his shoulder at me with that strange smile.

At last, I get it. He's not leering. He's congratulating me. He thinks I am with child, he thinks I walk slowly like this because I am about to give birth.

At last, he leaves; I am alone. Overhead, seagulls wheel in the sky.

"WHAT WAS HE like?" David asked early on, about my father whom he only got to meet that one time, that night of our first date.

We were hiking around a lake when David asked, while overhead a hawk circled.

"Like me," I said. "Like once we hiked this same trail and saw that same hawk…okay, not the *same* hawk, but one like it, and we sat in silence and watched it circling higher and higher until it disappeared into the whiteness of the sky. And then we hiked home."

"I'm not like that," David said. "I've already watched that hawk long enough. Is that okay?"

"Of course," I said, and we hiked on but now I think of my father again, his honesty, his humor, his capacity for sitting still in nature. I think about the time he expressed doubt about his faith, the two of us alone at the dining room table, my mother washing dishes in the kitchen, the other three children scattered. I was visiting from college, it was clear I'd lost my faith, that it wasn't a matter of finding the right priest, that I would never be confirmed. Still, my mother had hope. In a moment, she would hear him and rush into the room. She would whisk him away to their bedroom where I would for the first time hear them in serious argument, and then he would return and say it would be better for him to work out his doubts about his own faith in private. But for these few minutes, he was still talking. "It's the word *dominion* in the bible that bothers me," he was saying. "That word seems arrogant and dangerous. Dominion seems to put us at the top of a hierarchy of nature, and I'm not sure we *are* at the top," he went on. "I think maybe we're all just part of nature…"

ANOTHER DAY, ANOTHER hike. David's right to persuade me. Going into nature feels necessary now. We go up this time: deep blue sky, lush green hills beginning to flash the golden heat of summer. As I hike, I am narrating to myself, without even realizing I am, narrating to myself what is happening; and then my narration shifts suddenly to a vision of a book cover: *Silvan, Silvain, Silvano*. As the endorphins kick in, I begin to feel triumphant, as if the creation of a child out of words is as good as the creation of a child out of flesh. As if the redemption in our suffering will come from the giving of Silvan to the world in the form of a book. *Silvan, Silvain, Silvano: My Translatable Child*. My life, Silvan's life, will have been made worthwhile if I can give him to others in words. Then I hear my deluded chant and can't go on.

I throw myself to the ground.

I'm on all fours, staring at the ground. Inches from me is a patch of wild chamomile. Rising from the fuzzy green are little yellow flower-balls that sway at the tops of their stalks like tree-tops in a silly, powder-puff forest. When was the last time I observed a patch of weeds this carefully? The sun warms my back. David waits.

If he worries that other hikers will come along and observe my freakish grief, he says nothing. But at the same time, he has temporarily run out of consolation. He seems almost to have run out of tears. He's impatient now with my need to stop for every wave of grief. He stands higher up the hill from me, hunched in his gray fleece and jiggling one leg the way he does when he's anxious to get moving again, looking back and forth between my prostrate form and the yellow scar of path that disappears around a corner up ahead. He is enduring his grief by keeping busy, by consulting outside doctors, dealing with insurance, filling the car with gas while I am left free to feel every ripple of emotion. The postpartum hormones coursing through me amplify my grief, make it come in waves that bowl me over. But I can't stay like this all day. I can't sustain this drama. The feeling is passing. The need to be prostrate is gone. There is nothing to do but go on.

I heave myself upright.

We climb.

From A to Z

FOR DAYS HIS EYELIDS HAVE BEEN TWITCHING, BUT ON
the tenth day, they spring open. It's only for a second, but long
enough to see that bright flash of life. Dr. A has warned us this
might happen. Knowing Silvan's waking might confuse us,
he has assured us that even if the swelling goes down enough for
Silvan to revive, the brain damage will remain. At the same time,
Dr. A has reminded us that he himself is going off service and a
new doctor coming in.

"But you will like him. I have fully briefed him. He is very
compassionate."

Compassionate. How I cling to that word the first time Dr.
Z rushes in. I am holding Silvan, chatting with my mother across
the room, looking down occasionally to admire those newly-
opened eyes. Dr. Z stirs up the gloom, all smiles and efficient
energy. He says, "I'm going to conduct an exam of the baby now,"
lingering on the "a" as if to make the very word cute. This is how
the nurses used to talk about Silvan. Before they adjusted. Now
I am suspicious of anyone whose voice does not admit a touch of
pain, a sadness to their vowels. Silvan hardly moves, he never
makes a sound, but those long-lashed, hazel eyes seem to look
around. How pleased I am to see those eyes again.

An exam means relinquishing my baby, and I do so reluc-
tantly to this sweet-talking stranger. "Oh, you've got some
strength there," he says to Silvan; and, "good reflex." With each
bit of praise, my heart leaps with pride, but what for? For having

carried a baby to healthy term? For the little strength he has left? For the automatic reflexes? The beating heart? Is the doctor trying to torment me with hope? Is he saying Silvan might improve? At last Dr. Z turns to me. "Do you think he's particularly sleepy right now? I know I took him straight from your arms." "Oh, no" I say. "That's him wide awake." I laugh nervously, laugh with the agony that my son, wide-awake, his hazel eyes sliding languorously from side to side, seems to the doctor to be asleep.

Dr. Z lifts Silvan's little arms and pulls gently up. Silvan's chest lifts, his cleft chin tilts up, but the black-haired back of his little head barely clears the mattress. Gently Dr. Z lowers Silvan back down. "He should have used his neck strength to bring his head level with his shoulders."

But he's asleep, I want to say. *Let me wake him properly.* Motherly pride wants Silvan to pass this simple-seeming test.

"So do you want to talk here or go to a conference room?" Dr. Z asks. There is no question: a conference room, away from my mother who now picks Silvan up. I don't trust this guy in front of my mother. I know what she's thinking: *Silvan is praiseworthy. The nice new doctor has said so. The doctors last week were wrong. My prayers have been answered. The miracle has happened. He is revived.* I know, because I'm tempted to think the same.

So here we are again, back in the old Bad News Room, back in the same two chairs. The only difference is that this time Silvan's chart is enormous; at least two hundred pages fill his three ring binder. Dr. Z begins by telling us Silvan's story, his untroubled labor, the meconium present at birth, the lethargy, the initial diagnosis of subdural hematoma – as if we have not been living this story right along with Silvan – then the EEG showing something worse. Dr. Z is like the neurologist with her pearl earrings, presenting a detailed case out of fear of getting to the heart of the matter. He has big white teeth like silent piano keys that he licks as he talks.

Then, I hear him say, "We don't know if he can hear but we will test for that before he goes home with you."

Suddenly, my brain is in high gear; like a mother lifting a car to release her trapped child, my brain is cutting through the bullshit to save my son. "Why on earth would you perform more tests on my son," I ask, "if there is a DNR on him?"

"Oh," Dr. Z says, flipping through the chart. "You're right. You're right. I'm sorry. We would not be testing his hearing in that case."

"I thought you knew about this case?" I say. Hadn't he begun the meeting by saying he had been thoroughly debriefed? In retrospect, couldn't I almost hear resentment in his voice that Dr. A had taken so much time passing on this case? I am shocked. "You will like him," Dr. A had said.

"My mistake," he says, "I hadn't got that far in the chart."

I say, "You know, it was painful for me to watch you perform that exam on him, praising him as if he were a normal baby." I want to be honest with him, to show him that I have the fragile emotions of any mother with a child in hospital, only my emotions are reversed. Even if Silvan's eyes are open, his prognosis has not changed. Or has it? I need to know for sure, for if it hasn't changed, then even with his open eyes I still believe he should be allowed to die.

"I had to make my own assessment," he says. He licks his teeth.

"So what *is* your assessment?" David asks.

Dr. Z looks surprised, as if we should have known by watching. "Even without the EEG results, just from that physical exam, there were alarm bells ringing." Alarm bells. At last, we are coming to the same page. At last, he will confirm the prognosis on which we have made our decision. But instead he goes on, "I had a terminal patient once whose parents took him home. At home, he lasted six months."

I gasp. "Is it actually possible to survive six months without food?"

"No, they were feeding him, and happy for every minute they had."

"But we aren't feeding our child," I remind him.

"Are you saying," David asks, "that you want us to take him home so you can have his bed?"

THOUGH DR. Z assures us that we are welcome to keep Silvan in the hospital as long as we need, by that evening we have a new problem. Silvan has woken up enough to want to suck. I figure this out when he wriggles in my arms, makes a little noise, seems to be fussing in a mild, damaged way. Not wanting him to suffer, I offer him my finger, and to my surprise he sucks it and is soothed.

That night on the way home from the hospital, the midnight streets dark and deserted – each night, it seems, we stay later and later – David asks, "Should we tell Dr. Z?" I look over at him. David's face is ghastly, pale with exhaustion, lips stretched in a grimace.

"I don't know, I don't know," I say.

David begins to weave in the lane, trying not to cry.

Though we want to believe this is all just part of the waking up that Dr. A had warned us about, with David's question, we sense we are crossing a new ethical line. Not feeding Silvan now may no longer be as justifiable as it was when he could only eat artificially. With an adult who stops eating as death approaches, an argument can be made for not forcing them to eat against their will, but babies always have to be fed by someone else even when healthy. I find that the mother in me wants to believe that if Silvan can now suck, then he can eat, and if he can eat then perhaps he needs to be offered food. As in one of my childhood fantasies about sainthood, I want to believe if I only love him enough, he will learn to eat, go off to school, get Bs and Cs. I could write a book then about the heroism of my defiance of Western Medicine, the astonishing power of a mother's faith. In fact, each time I peek at the newspapers stacked unread at home, I find these kinds of stories featured – it seems our newspaper is in the midst of a series on babies who have "miraculously" survived – but I refuse to be seduced. Silvan is not a baby who can "recover" if I simply have the right kind of hope. To think this would be to flatter myself at *his* expense.

BY THE NEXT morning, our secret is out. The nurses know Silvan can suck; they know that when you stick a finger in his mouth, he is soothed. How relieving to know that the nurses are so good here, paying as much attention to our son as we are, soothing him with their own fingers. "Did you already know?" asks the one who gives us the news, and when I nod, she says, "Of course you did. You're his mother." In this way, we are saved from our own secret.

That afternoon, Dr. Z comes in to talk about the sucking. "There has been a change in status" is how he puts it.

"What does that mean for us?" I ask.

"Whenever there's a change in status, we have to review the course of treatment."

Though he speaks in medical jargon, I think I know what he means and for a moment I am in that tunnel again, at the bottom of that well down which I fell when I first heard the news that Silvan was damaged. The future I want for my son is being yanked from me again. But then I remember this is not just something I feel in my gut; I have the language of the hospital to explain myself. Although I want to believe that Silvan might be able to eat, I still believe that he should be allowed to die because his prognosis has not changed. I say, "But the change in status doesn't change his prognosis, does it?"

"No," Dr. Z admits.

"With this prognosis, we don't think he should have to live."

"In that case," he says, "we need to convene a meeting of the ethics committee."

We don't know what an ethics committee is and he explains, in brief, that it is a panel – of doctors, nurses, ethicists, legal counsel, lay people from the community – that has to be convened to give recommendations whenever there is a question about the course of treatment.

"Is that because you disagree with this course of treatment?" David asks.

Dr. Z repeats, "We do this whenever there is a question about a course of treatment."

"But why, if you agree with us?" David asks.

Dr. Z does not say specifically if he agrees or disagrees. "I am not comfortable continuing this course of treatment without a review from the ethics committee."

We feel at sea. This struggle has been there between us since his very first exam of Silvan. But it is always like this, strangely submerged. He is the only person in the hospital who seems to disagree with us and we want to get purchase on the ground and do battle with him, but everything feels slippery. I think of my father again. With what dignity he approached his dying, as if this were his last lesson to me. I was twenty-eight; he was sixty-one. He'd been given one year. "We've decided I'll retire," he said, "and go through the treatments, and then we'll go on one last trip to Poland because we loved it so much there last time." He got dressed the next morning and went off to work and named a successor at the lab where he'd been chief for over twenty years, a visionary scientist butting heads with state bureaucracy over lead in children's playgrounds, bad air in buildings, passive smoking. He came home with a crumpled stack of reusable brown-paper lunch bags from the stash in his desk drawers. He made it into work perhaps five more times, and then he got too sick from the treatments to go anywhere. But he remained himself. He made the nurses in the hospital laugh. He called his catheter bag full of piss his "Gucci bag." And once, when they were all acting as though he still had a year, a nurse tried to teach him how to walk with a walker. "Push it like a grocery cart," she said. And my weak and trembling father started going haywire, rolling sideways with the walker, then lurching to a stop and swearing. "What's wrong?" she asked in a panic, trying to grab his arm and keep him stable. "You said push it like a grocery cart," he said, "so this one has a wonky wheel." I remember my father, struggling as we are now, with his own doctor. "Once your fever's down..." the doctor would say, "we can try this new treatment or..." At last it was my father who held the compass, who headed home with hospice, my father who recognized that it was time to die.

"Of course, it may be difficult," Dr. Z says now, "to convene the members of the committee so quickly, by tomorrow, or the next day at the latest..."

"Why by tomorrow?" David asks.

"I won't continue this course of treatment over the weekend without a review."

"But what if you can't get everyone together soon enough?" I say. I am in agony. I picture Silvan hooked back up to his machines. Fed again for a weekend. Hasn't he already had his life prolonged enough to prove that dying is what he's supposed to do?

Battles

ETHICS COMMITTEES, SO COMMON IN HOSPITALS NOW, were almost non-existent prior to the 1970s. It was not until Karen Ann Quinlan's coma and the subsequent legal battles that the necessity of such forums became apparent. The absence of ethics committees prior to Quinlan is in part because, until the 1960s, the decisions doctors made for their dying patients were simpler. But with new technologies, patients could be pushed to the edge of what some would consider life. This is just as true for babies now as it has been for years for adults. While the age at which a fetus is considered viable has gotten younger, interventions have also become more extreme. How many stories there are about babies who have been saved. How heartening those stories. And how hidden and underreported the other story – that of children who go on to live on the tortured edge between life and death for years. Back when I was born, severely premature babies were called miscarriages. And a baby born as listless as Silvan might even have been classified a "stillbirth."

When I first read this fact, that Silvan might at one time have been called "stillborn," I experience both relief and shock. Back then, it was not uncommon for such "stillborn" babies to be starved. With the father in the waiting room and the mother in her twilight haze, the doctor would make the decision alone. He would decide what was best for the family, what would make it easier to go on and have more children. "Your baby did not make it," he'd tell the parents while the baby lay hidden from them in a bassinet. The nurses would be told not to touch it. This fact is both shocking and affirming. While it makes me feel ill to think of Silvan dying without my knowledge and alone, how much easier it would've been in some ways to think Silvan had simply "not made it." How much more like nature, cruel and efficient.

There are reasons doctors made more of these decisions in the past. In the past, doctors tended to know their patients well, sometimes since birth. They paid house calls, they knew their patients' families and lifestyles, they could make decisions that fit the patient's sense of life and death. But these days, medical treatment and technology change so rapidly that there are more specialists to consult, and our personal doctors are less reliable, more dependent on whatever health insurance we are lucky enough to have. For many, the family unit is also less stable, fewer patients belong to a church or a cultural group with distinct beliefs and rituals around death. The choices to be made are now more complex.

In such a climate, the need for patients to have individual authority has increased. We want to have the final say on what happens to our own bodies – or, in the case of our children, what happens to theirs – since there are so many options. We have a patients' bill of rights. But doctors, too, have autonomy. They also have their code of ethics. And when the patients' and the doctors' codes of ethics come into conflict, there has to be a formal place to come together to make a decision, a place to simulate the community that used to help with such decisions in the past. It is not a ruling body, but a body that gives recommendations. There are codes of ethics they may follow, but each case is different in its specificity. In the case of a baby like Silvan who has lived too little of life to have an opinion about death, it is the lives of the parents that have to be looked to in order to make a decision. Only if no agreement can be reached does a case end up in the courts.

But we don't understand yet what the ethics committee is

for and so the time between Dr. Z telling us that he is requesting a meeting and the time that it happens – though it spans only a few days – stretches horribly.

IN A FRENZY of anxiety, we ask friends for referrals to other hospitals. We contact the director of a pediatric ward in another major hospital who says that his hospital would agree with our decision and that he could have Silvan transferred there. He is very nice, reassuring, reasonable. We also talk to a nurse in his hospital who runs one of the first palliative care wings for children to be built in a hospital in this country. She says that we don't actually need to be transferred. She says she can arrange to have us sent home with one of the rare hospice organizations that works with children. That way we won't have to continue feeling that we are at odds with our doctor while retaining some institutional support.

We try to tell Dr. Z how anxious we are. But he's been vague enough in his answers about convening the meeting that when he says, "This is not about antagonism," we can't believe him.

Not even Dr. A can help. We run into him one day. Though he is not on service anymore, there he is rushing down a hospital corridor. He knows about the ethics committee meeting. In that usual, straightforward and empathetic way that we take such comfort in, he says, "You should not think of this as a battle. This is for you, so that everyone agrees…"

"But Dr. Z *doesn't* agree with us," we say.

"You don't know that," he says. "All you know is that he is not comfortable proceeding without this meeting."

"But what does that mean 'he is not comfortable'?"

"You should not think of this as a battle. This is for you…"

Dr. A repeats in his soothing voice, and we are disappointed that even he has abandoned us. We cannot hear what he is saying. We suspect everyone of duplicity, we hear only platitudes.

BEFORE THE MEETING, David researches the tenets of medical ethics. "Here they are," he says, "beneficence, non-maleficence, autonomy, and justice."

"Great," I say. "And how does that help?"

He tries to explain. "Beneficence means you should do what benefits the patient. Non-maleficence means you should not harm the patient. Autonomy means you should respect the patient's wishes. Justice means you should treat all patients equally, which includes allocating resources equitably."

"And how does that help?" I repeat. I know he's finding this research somewhat soothing. I know that he and I are different because he is a man and I am a woman, or because we're just different people, but his insistence on these four terms is bewildering. We are sitting at the dining room table, picking at dinner. We are fed by friends. Every night someone else drops off a different meal so that all we have to do is lift our forks while we figure out what to do about Silvan, or rush to return to the hospital to hold him. We've unpacked nothing since his birth. Whatever I took to the hospital during labor lies against the walls, still stuffed inside those plastic bags stamped with large blue letters that read: Patient Belongings. Those belongings are indeed patient as they lie against the wall, but there is no room in my mind for unpacking them; no room for cooking, nor for anything not related to Silvan.

David begins to define the terms again, but it all sounds so contradictory – which it is. What benefits Silvan might also harm him, what is good for him might not be good for others. Because of such conflicts between terms, the right medical decisions are not always obvious. "How would you even use those terms to make our case?" I ask.

He says, "I don't know. All I can think about is my cousin and how much her parents have suffered over her."

I know what he means. It took years for them to tease apart the various problems that have added up to her developmental delay, years to figure out what services she could receive to make her life manageable, years even to communicate with her calmly. She is now an adult living hours away in a publicly-funded group home; they spend the bulk of their free time driving back and forth to see her. I know they must worry about her future once they are gone. And I know that they love her. I push away my plate, suddenly disgusted with David. "But you can't say that, can you? I mean, that's selfish."

"But people aren't isolated. They belong to a community," he says.

I agree with him about community, but I am angry now. I remember his early doubts about my ability to mother well. Who is the selfish one now? "Whenever you get pregnant," I say righteously, "you never know what you're going to get, or how much you're going to have to sacrifice."

" I know," David says. "That's always scared me."

"So what are you saying? That you've changed your mind about having a child now that we have one?"

"So what are you saying?" he says. "I mean, you can't do this for me. If we want to stay married, we both have to believe this is right."

Both of our plates are now pushed away, our appetites gone.

After a moment of silence, David goes on. "It's true," he admits, "I worry about being selfish, about trying to get out of taking care of him. Don't you?" He tries to take my hand across the table.

"God no!" I say, ignoring that hand. "I think it would be selfish of us to keep him alive. I mean, a part of me would just like to keep him with me always, smelling his sweet head and knowing I'm being good by taking care of him, but I think that would be wrong for him so I am sacrificing what I want for his sake."

" You wouldn't really want to do that," David persists softly, earnestly. " You wouldn't really want to devote your life to him, would you?"

In this moment, how grateful I am to have married him. With his honesty, he is not just insulting my Day-Glo headscarf or my potential for motherhood anymore, he's asking me to examine my deepest most secret self. I take his hand. Perhaps he's right. Though I know I have it in me to mother Silvan as much as he needs, perhaps a part of this decision *is* selfish, perhaps I am just as relieved as David that my life from here on out can be spared round-the-clock vigilance for an incapacitated son. I hang on to that hand.

"Maybe you're right," I say. "Maybe I just like imagining that I'm sacrificing my desire to keep him alive for his sake. Maybe I'm lying to myself."

As soon as I admit as much, the honesty makes everything clear. How lucky we are that this makes sense to us on all levels. We believe that Silvan should be allowed to die not only for his sake but for all of ours.

Chance of Regret

ON SILVAN'S TWELFTH DAY, THE ETHICS COMMITTEE meeting takes place in the basement of the hospital. What David and I are doing, we will later learn, is unusual. Prior to us, few parents have made this particular choice in this particular hospital. In a strange reversal from the time of Karen Ann Quinlan, most parents who come to ethics committees these days come to fight for the right to a miracle. But we are unaware of how we may be fitting into the arc of medical history; we simply have a feeling between us and are hoping we will have the language to express it.

Sister C leads us there from Silvan's room, David, David's father Larry, and me. David wants Larry there as a third, calmer witness to the proceedings. Sister C has lost her soothing tone in favor of a lighthearted efficiency. As she leads us into the bowels of the building, she banters about the latest improvements to the hospital. She leads us down corridors and into elevators and eventually into a large, windowless room. Despite fluorescent lighting, the room recedes before us into gloom. In front of us: three empty chairs. Seated around the conference table beyond our chairs, maybe twenty people, though it seems like more. We recognize almost no one. There is Silvan's sweet nurse Kerry, and an intern we know, Sister C, and of course, Dr. Z. The rest are a blur of suits and skirts. They are all silent, waiting.

The director of the ethics committee is a familiar-looking, older woman with graying, tousled hair. That helps. She invites us to sit. Friendly but businesslike, she introduces herself and asks everyone else at the table to introduce themselves one by one.

David has a pen and paper with which he draws a diagram of the table, where each person sits, who each person is – Dr. Z, Nurse Kerry, a medical ethicist, legal counsel, a lay person whose child once died in this hospital. David is still convinced that this will be a grueling debate and that he will need to know who his allies are, who his enemies.

I, on the other hand, am beginning to believe Dr. Z that this is for us. Considering my love for Silvan, it seems impossible that they will disagree. The night before, rounding the corner to our street after leaving Silvan at the hospital for the night, I felt my love for him rearing up inside of me on its hind legs like a bear with claws extended. No one can force me to make my baby suffer life.

Introductions over, it is our turn.

Despite his preparations, David is without a speech. He turns to me. "Do you want to start?" Yes! With that beast of love reared up inside me, I say, "No one in this room could want to feed my son as much as I do." In my breasts, I feel stirring whatever milk remains.

Now what? I think.

I have to stop and catch my breath, blow my nose. On the other side of David, Larry realizes he will not be the calm witness after all. Like everyone else, he will later tell me, he is tearing up. But at the time, I'm unaware of other people's emotions. I am aware only of my own words, that cocoon I need to weave around my son.

Without a speech prepared, I tilt between instinct and intellect. At last, I go with intellect. "What we don't know, however, is if he could eat if he tried. He seems to be sucking, but we don't know if he can coordinate sucking with swallowing and gagging. So it's possible he could choke and die. Or, if he can't protect his airway, that he'll get pneumonia and die. Or that he'll only be able to eat enough to prolong his starvation, which I think would be worse. And somewhere down the road, even if he can learn to eat, we'll have to make another decision. What if he gets pneumonia, or if his seizures return, or he stops breathing again? Where's the line? When's enough? So far he hasn't even known the discomfort of eating, gagging, gas, poopy diapers. All he's known in life is love. Since he came into the world through love, since he's been surrounded by it, I'd like him to leave knowing nothing else but love... "

Go on, I think, *go on*. I feel as though I've only made an introduction here, given the background. My voice has ended on an uptone, expecting more facts, more persuasive logic, something to come out, but then I hear my final word: love.

It is not everything, of course. I feel deceptive for not having strayed beyond my love for Silvan, afraid to lose the argument if I appear to care for anyone but him. And yet, what is the difference between Silvan and me? The lines between us are still blurry, fresh as he is from my womb. When I close my eyes for a nap, I still feel that I am him. When I touch my face, I'm startled to find my own nose there. And anyway, in the incredible way of our marriage in this crisis, David is taking up where I left off. "I know firsthand what it's like to have a developmentally delayed child in the family," he begins. "My first cousin was born with a range of developmental problems, and I've seen how much her parents have had to struggle to raise her, the suffering of that family."

I am afraid. Indeed, there is fresh movement around the room. Questions. About his cousin's diagnosis. And what exactly constitutes parental suffering.

"It sounds selfish, but a part of me is relieved," David goes on, "that Silvan is as damaged as he is so that we can make this choice for him. Because if he was less damaged, of course we would take care of him. But I know what a toll that can take on a marriage, and on subsequent children, and on the whole community."

There is a nodding of heads. People seem to understand

that Silvan is part of a larger community. What a relief this is. How much larger it makes Silvan himself that he is part of this larger family.

Now David is done and it's time for general questions.

First, someone asks if we understand that no prognosis is a hundred percent certain.

"Yes," I say, "but this one is certain enough that I would not want to gamble for a miracle and have Silvan suffer more because of it."

Dr. Z sits forward then and I stiffen. Will he say that we have to be more certain? Will he say that we always have to gamble on the side of life? After all, this is what some Christians say, as if staying alive is the greatest good, as if the longer we stay alive, the more likely we are to get to heaven. Instead, he says, "Do you have the support of your whole family in this decision?" For once, he is not using medical language. For once, he is not disagreeing. For once, he seems interested in us. Still I'm suspicious. Perhaps he thinks I'll be defensive and say, "Of course everyone agrees with us," and then he will know I've closed down real conversation. How wrong he is. I think of my father, home with hospice, trying to sit through a family dinner with a neck brace on because he hardly had the strength to chew let alone to keep his head upright. Food kept running down his chin onto the cream-colored foam, until at last he turned to a friend of mine who was trying not to gawk at the pathetic scene, and teased her, "If you ever want to write about this, check with Monica first. I'm giving her the story." After dinner, he gave me a stamp, "To start mailing out your writing," he said. I think of my mother who married such a man, a man so honestly funny and kind even in his dying. How much I love her for marrying him. For her own honesty and generosity. Her tolerance of ambiguity. Her support. I look at Dr. Z triumphantly. "Not everyone in our family would necessarily make this choice for their own child, but they all support us."

Sister C weighs in then, as if to counterbalance Dr. Z. "Any decision born of love is the right decision," she says.

It is a lovely sentiment, though I doubt it's always true. But no one scoffs at her because love, I suppose, is part of what we're doing here. This committee is listening to the quality of our love, making sure that they recognize it as love, and that our actions are consistent with that love. This committee is not just about science and facts.

The mother whose child died tells us we are brave and unusual for coming here with this argument on behalf of our child.

Nurse Kerry agrees. "I'm learning a lot from you," she says, "from watching you love Silvan." She likes the boom box we've brought in for Silvan. She turns on music so she can dance with him around his room.

Then the ethicist asks if we are clear that euthanasia is illegal. What we are doing is not euthanasia. What we are doing is stopping a treatment that is futile – in this case, feeding – because feeding will not change the grimness of his prognosis, it will not keep him from dying of his condition.

"Yes," we say.

He reminds us that morphine does not hasten death – *it only palliates a death that is already coming*.

Yes, we say, we understand.

We understand and yet we don't. We know Silvan has been trying to die since birth, through seizures, through forgetting to breathe. We know he should be allowed to die again. And yet, how is it that not feeding him is more compassionate than euthanasia? Why can we withdraw his food but not let him die in other ways? Later I will learn that this ethicist is a Catholic priest. Later, I will learn that the Catholic Church has been at the forefront of this issue for hundreds of years, providing much of our legal understanding of the balance between preserving life at all cost and considering the quality of that life. For the church, biological life is considered a "good," but not the highest good. According to the church, we are sacred not just for having bodies, but for having a relationship to those around us. Later, I will learn how our own advances in medicine have created a field of medical ethics out of what used to be a purely religious debate. I will also learn first-hand how ethicists may be able to navigate issues in the abstract while never living with the consequences, ethicists who might actually be made "queasy," as one put it, by the details resulting from allowing Silvan to die while agreeing that it was a moral act. I think Silvan should be allowed to die, but is this a good death? On this day, we are too overwhelmed for such probing. On this day, we're only looking for agreement on a decision that feels right for our son.

The director of the committee is now saying, "You will be relieved to know that this committee agrees unanimously with your decision. You've shown great understanding," she goes on, "of Silvan's diagnosis and prognosis. You clearly understand the challenges of caring for a child who would require around-the-clock monitoring for whatever remains of his life. And because feeding would only prolong a suffering you do not want for him and would not want for yourselves in the same situation, we agree with you that feeding is futile. So long as you understand that we cannot and will not practice euthanasia, we agree to proceed with the current course of treatment, including comfort care."

Again, we say we understand.

Then David wants to know if there could be any change that would force us to come back to an ethics committee meeting.

"No," she says.

"Not even if Silvan starts speaking in full sentences?" I ask. Though I joke, I can't help thinking this is possible in some dream world; I am relieved when people laugh.

Dr. Z does not laugh. He's not quite done. He leans forward, licks his teeth and says, "Is there any chance that someday you'll regret your decision?"

Holding Silvan

ONLY NURSES WHO AGREE WITH OUR CHOICE FOR SILVAN
work with him. Perhaps these nurses aren't supposed to tell us
how they feel personally, but now that we have public approval,
more of them seem free to speak to us and this is helpful. One
maternal-looking nurse with her hair up in a bun tells us that for
seventeen years on this floor, she never questioned her job. For
seventeen years, she accepted that her job was to save lives until
the day she tried working at an institution for children whose
lives had been saved. She no longer believes it is in the best interest of *all* children to be saved.

"They suffer," she says.

This is the refrain. "They suffer. They suffer."

"They suffer," says a nurse who sometimes works with children a floor above ours, children who spend their lives in and
out of hospitals. She also knows from personal experience. As a
delivery nurse, she'd once delivered a baby whose mother died
in childbirth. Over time, she'd fallen in love with and married
the widower and taken such meticulous care of his brain-damaged baby that the baby survived until twenty-one. "He was
considered high-functioning because he was able to roll."

This really sticks with us: "able to roll."

"He did know us so there was that," she says, "but his only
real pleasure was eating, eating also being a higher function.
His favorite food was ice cream." But it was hard to feed him, she
went on. It was her full-time job. Often she had to insert a

feeding tube anyway. And eventually, despite the fancy wheel-chairs and physical therapy and constant attention, he was terribly ill and it was discovered that his spinal deformation was cutting off his duodenum and this was the reason for his increasing pain and illness. Her own pain is obvious. "We had to starve him to death then, at twenty-one."

Another nurse says, "I would do what you are doing for my own child."

Another simply crouches at my feet, clasping my knees. "Let it out, let it out," she says as I sob.

NEEDING SOMETHING TO occupy his mind besides Silvan, David becomes good at guessing at the problems of babies around us. For example, one day there is a new baby. We can see him easily from Silvan's room. He is a big baby. Must be a term baby. Already on artificial ventilation. And here comes the woman who did Silvan's EEG, the one who was evasive. As she did with Silvan, she attaches electrodes all over the baby's head and stares at her computer screen for twenty minutes. David overhears a nurse describe the EEG as "flat." A very young woman shows up in a wheelchair then, looking dazed. Since the nurses are setting up a screen for privacy, we figure he's about to die. It's all happening very fast. We go on a break, and when we return the young mother is being wheeled away and her baby is gone.

I want to tell her that I empathize, but whatever I mumble comes out wrong, for she stares straight through me, stricken.

Her baby is dead whereas mine is still alive.

"IT'S HARDEST ON the nurses," Nurse Kerry says, "when the parents aren't involved. At least with Silvan you can see that he is loved, but with those babies, it's the nurses who do all the work..."

"Does it make you want to hold those babies less?"

"You want to hold them more," Kerry says. She tells us about one baby born without a brain at all. Those parents simply left the baby to die and never came back. "That was hard," she says, "because when the nurse picked her up, she didn't react at all."

Is a baby with no brain even human? I don't know, but I feel ill. I can't imagine leaving Silvan. I can only imagine letting him leave us.

"TELL HIM THAT you love him and will be okay if he leaves," Father B once said. "Tell him you're ready." Hospice had warned us that it would be a day or two at most, but the priest seemed to know to the minute when my father would go. How familiar this seemed, the priest summoned, the family gathered, how familiar from old paintings, and from the story Maggy had told me in college of her mother holding out for Easter; it is the good death that many of us used to aspire to. As we settled in a circle around his bed, my father searched our faces one by one, and the pale blue of his morphine-hazed eyes seemed anxious. Kim, only eighteen but somehow already wise about death, said, "I think he's looking for Mark."

"Mark is safe in heaven," my mother reassured my father.

My father relaxed, stopped his search, and closed his eyes.

Still he lay there breathing. On and on we sat. One breath, a pause, one breath.

Then Kim said, "It's okay, Daddy, you can go."

After the next breath, he was gone. His body sank and stilled like clay while just above the surface something skimmed, a sense of breath, of light.

MY MOTHER, WHO slept each night next to my father in his rented hospital bed, my mother who would do anything I ask of her for Silvan, worries that our love is only prolonging this agony. Silvan is now over two weeks old. Perhaps, she suggests, we shouldn't keep holding him so much if we really want him to go. Perhaps our holding him is keeping him alive.

This may be true, but it's what I want, it's what seems right for Silvan, and the nurses back me up. All day long we hold him;

and at night, a nurse tells us, they vie for him on their shift. From nurse to nurse he is passed, nestled in the crooks of arms, as the nurses go about their work. "So you're the mother of the beautiful baby," a nurse says to me one morning, craning her neck to see me from the other end of the long sink where David and I and a bunch of nurses are all scrubbing our hands and arms. "No wonder he's so cute," she says, which is about the sweetest thing anyone has said until now, because it's so normal.

Another normal thing the nurses suggest is that we take him outside, away from the stale air and constant light and noise. After all, he's never been outside. They describe the hospital courtyard with its beautiful trees. Unlike some hospitals, this hospital has no palliative care ward. It's designed only for babies they're still trying to save; but they want to help, to make this dying as good as it can be.

The courtyard we find is a ring of backless benches around a u-shaped driveway; it faces a three-story helicopter landing pad. Hospital employees come out there to smoke and helicopters land with a deafening racket, and the grass is almost always too wet to sit on. Over time, it will depress us. But the first time we take Silvan from his room, we feel giddy and alive. We free him from his monitors (only monitors for his heart rate and temperature now, attached by sticky pads, "So he won't, you know," one most honest nurse admits, "die alone") and we wrap him snugly and walk out of there.

He feels so small in my arms, so manageable, so mine.

As we pass other parents with babies still hooked to machines, they look up at us with distant smiles. Dr. A had wanted us in our own little room so we wouldn't envy the other parents taking babies home. But Silvan is the only baby I want and I have him, right now, in my arms. I want to tell them, "Don't envy us. He's dying," and yet I'm bursting with pleasure and pride. It's a crazy feeling. I'm triumphant. I'm ecstatic. Mother and child, we stop passing strangers in their tracks. "Oh look at you," they coo.

Breaking Plates

WE KNOW THAT PEOPLE REALLY WANT TO HELP, TO BE a part of this dying, to love Silvan now while they can alongside us. David even stumbles across a discussion online about how best to help when a baby is dying. From the details, he realizes the discussion is actually about *us*, and how *we* can be helped. Because the only help I think I need is to have Silvan held, we check the box at the front desk allowing anyone to come and see him and *everyone* comes: neighbors, coworkers, the receptionist of our chiropractor.

My friend Eve flies out from the East Coast to help with the love that people want to give us. I've known Eve almost as long as Maggy Brown. Eve is a talker. She likes to ask questions, to probe. I like how she coaxes my interior world into the light, but I don't think I can be probed right now without pain. I don't want her to pain me. I can't afford for this crisis to damage our friendship, to be disappointed by her. I will need to love her and be loved by her when Silvan is gone.

So, after Eve has come straight from the airport to hold Silvan, I ask her to stay not with us but with mutual friends who set her up with a phone. Eve's gift to me will be to call everyone I know, to pore through my address book, contacting people so that I won't have to endure the awkwardness of telling people who don't know – a month, two months, ten years from now – what has happened. She talks and talks, tells the story over and over.

She draws my friends and acquaintances around us, giving them a chance to help.

Other people offer to fly across the country, across the world, to help. I'm careful in selecting people, and in giving them jobs. My friend who still hasn't told me her marriage is crumbling comes out and takes David to the grocery store. David holds Silvan and sings to him – he has a whole repertoire of songs with his own lyrics suited for Silvan by now; he sings "You are My Sunshine" with Silvan's name in place of "sunshine" – but he can't possibly hold Silvan for as long as I can. He's hungry for some normal activity after all these weeks away from work, and I'm eager to be left alone to do nothing but hold Silvan more. Standing beside my love for Silvan, all other love seems dwarfed, so I send my friend off with David, in this way tending to my relationships without turning from my son.

Next my sister calls from Brazil in a crisis of indecision about whether to come now or after Silvan is dead, and I tell her she needs to get on a plane immediately. Katya has been known to go into a tailspin when she is unsure of something, and I dread that happening to her now. I tell her she needs to meet her nephew.

A few days later, Katya arrives and comes straight to the hospital from the airport. I walk into Silvan's room, and there she sits holding him, next to my mother. Katya looks up, her eyes and face aglow.

"What do you think of my baby?" I ask, the joyous words bursting from me, and I feel my mother flinch the way she does when her children's exuberance stumbles onto the set of what she considers a somber scene.

"He's sooo cute," Katya says.

For a moment, the sibling link is forged in gold.

The next day, Katya says, "Thanks for telling me to come. No one in Brazil was helpful. They were all saying, 'He'll be all right...' or 'I am praying...' They couldn't wrap their minds around doctors in America unable to save a baby."

"It wasn't just for you," I say, "Holding him is for all of us."

ONE PERSON WHO does not offer to help is our doula. She has been leaving messages that we still haven't answered until it occurs to David that she's anxious about her final payment. It is now almost three weeks since Silvan's birth and yet I balk at paying her. "She still owes us a post-partum visit," I say.

"You want her to visit?" David asks, surprised.

"No," I say, "I never want to see or speak to her again."

David says I'm being petty and irrational and calls her back; and when she hears that Silvan is still alive, she diplomatically says we don't have to pay her yet – but she does want to make sure that we keep the book she lent us safe, the book about the amazing brains of newborns. When he repeats this to me, my emotions flare again – "What about the *damaged* brains of newborns? Would she want a book back about that?" I rant – until I realize she has become the scapegoat for whatever rage or shame or blame I feel. She was there when Silvan was damaged. She was the one who suggested I stand in the shower without the fetal monitor. It was in the shower that I felt that big kick that may or may not have had anything to do with Silvan's damage. She did nothing wrong but she was there, and I have nowhere else to dump blame. I will give her back her book, I tell David, but only when she brings the photo of Silvan that she promised to take when he was born. If she expects to be paid, I expect her to face this death.

ANOTHER TARGET OF my irrational scorn is the hospital's social worker. Though she reported early on in her notes that we were dealing "as well as can be expected" and that we were "tender with each other," now she begins to say we are "resistant" to her help. Even as she enters the room, she seems scared of us. But what help can she give? She knows how to arrange for housing, transportation, how to negotiate with insurers. But we are lucky enough ("lucky," we keep calling ourselves) to live near the hospital, to have a working car, and good insurance through David's company that continues to support him in his absence. I glare at her when she persists in offering these few things. Worried about us, she passes us off to another social worker. However, this second social worker does not find us resistant. She finds us open to her. She says that when she asks, "How can I help?" we ask, "How can a social worker help with a baby who is dying?" and so she offers help in funeral arrangements, cremation, whatever we will need. I wonder how the first social worker could be so afraid of death and am relieved when I learn she's left this job for something less demanding.

FRIENDS DO LITTLE better against the rising tide of my rage and scorn. Our old friends Claudia and Brian say they can't come to the hospital. They're expecting their third child and Claudia says she's afraid she will "make a fool" of herself by crying too much.

Instead, they take turns talking to me by phone, mostly in complaint about their own lives – Claudia's ongoing morning sickness, Brian's commute, which keeps him away from the family for half the week, the fact that this third child has come so late into their lives that they'll old before it goes off to college. Perhaps they really are engrossed in their own suffering, or perhaps they are trying to commiserate in misery; either way it doesn't work. Maybe they simply disagree with our choice. After all, at the end of the conversation Brian asks, "Why don't you let him die of pneumonia or something else more natural?" There is no judgment in his voice, but I'm so startled to be questioned about a choice that's already been made that I hand the phone to David. And after they hang up, I don't dwell on Brian's question. Instead, I swell with my superior suffering, strutting for David in a rage that others "can't deal."

STILL SWOLLEN, STILL strutting with disappointment and rage, I make the bed for David's mother. She's the only grandparent who hasn't met Silvan and she's arriving from New Jersey for a week. She's hoping that she has timed it so that she can both meet Silvan and be here when he dies. In the best of times, Linda is loving and sympathetic but always she and David argue. They argue on the phone, too, but their arguments are worse in person. Sometimes David simply argues about her inability to argue well, how she says whatever comes into her mind. This week, Linda brings as fallback conversation her boycott of France. Though she considers herself a savvy liberal, we consider ourselves more liberal, more informed, better able to read between the lines; for us, her boycott of France is misguided. And yet, when David arrives with her from the airport, he tells me that for once he couldn't be bothered to argue politics. I take her suitcase down to her bedroom and tell her what time she will be able to visit with her grandson. I want her to be as obsessed with him as we are. I don't want her to fill the silence with other kinds of conversation.

The week passes with little change in Silvan. He will not die while Linda is here. David and I spend all of our time at the hospital while Linda is ferried around by my mother and David's sister, trying to fill the time she's not with us. So here we are on her last night, at the end of a long day at the hospital, sitting in the living room – Linda, my mother, David's sister – eating dinner in silence from plates on our laps. David and I have nothing to say beyond Silvan and no one else can think of anything appropriate to fill the gloom. Linda rocks back and forth, back and forth anxiously in the glider as if to fill the silence this way. Next to her foot on the rocking footstool lies her empty dinner plate. I watch the plate going back and forth, back and forth. I'm sure she'll break it. I consider getting up to move the plate to a more stable surface, but then I realize I'd rather have the haughty pleasure of having known she would break it. I suppose I want something to break; I want not only the triumph of having predicted that it would break but also to feel this petty pain and anger, because the pain of losing Silvan is anything but petty;

it is entirely unpredictable in its vastness. The strain of loving him is starting to take its toll.

So: I am already primed when Linda begins once again saying what a shame it is but she's never going to buy anything French again – wine, mustard, shoes – or even go to France for a visit, though she's always wanted to see Paris, and I lose it. I jump up. I say, "How dare you talk that way?"

"What way?" she asks.

"That hateful way. My French son…"

She stops rocking.

"With my French son dying in the hospital…"

"French?" she says, bewildered. "Your son is French?"

"Yes," I say, my voice rising as I stand up, "my son is French, and my son is Jewish…" After weeks of cramped stress, the expansive light inside my head is as uplifting as champagne. I am more than myself, I have transcended politics, borders, hatred. I feel as though my love for Silvan has transformed me into every mother who has ever lost a child in the history of the world, as if I have become Love itself, and in my heady delusion I say, "Get this *woman* out of my house!"

"Me?" she says, still bewildered, but my rage does not abate. If Linda's not going to break that plate, then something's got to break. David pulls me from the room. For once, he does not insist that I do the right thing. He does not insist that I go and apologize. He's used to my sudden rages, he's used to being the one who civilizes me in petty circumstances, at cocktail parties where someone says something I think too stupid and selfish to keep silent about and he tells me to go back and apologize. But now he seems to understand that I need to rage, that I need to be breaking things. That this is the visit where I will be the one to fight with his mother. That I need to feel righteous. He tells me to go to bed while he deals with her.

In the morning, Linda remains. Here she comes up from the guest room. She finds me in the kitchen alone where she offers to make her chicken soup to leave in our freezer before she returns to New Jersey. Would I like that? Sure, I say, noncommittally, knowing David would like it. She and David go off to the store and return with a chicken, a parsley root, some carrots, onion and dill, and while she shows me what she's putting in the pot, she says, "I'm sorry I upset you last night. I wasn't thinking."

"I'm sorry I tried to kick you out of the house," I say.

"I wasn't thinking either."

"I love you guys," she says, "and I just want to help."

I want to say I love her back, but the real and flawed love between a mother and her adult children is too distant and confusing to ponder. I feel as if my love for Silvan has been distilled into something so pure that what other people call "love" is a lie, a mere convenient word. And so I mumble, "Thanks," and it isn't until she has returned to New Jersey that I feel how hard this must be for her. To love a dying grandson from a distance. As Silvan's mother, I may be suffering the most over Silvan, but as his mother I'm also buffered from the pain.

He is in my arms for hours and hours. Seven inches is the distance between us, between my face and his. I can see him perfectly at seven inches away, but even my eyes are starting to betray me. If I sit and look at him for too long, when I look back up the world around me is a blur.

Seed Pearls

IT GETS WORSE. AS THE FAT LEAVES HIS BODY, SILVAN reveals a different face. In his third week, he looks like a miniature boy of five or six. He has high cheekbones and a pointed chin, and papery eyelids that are usually closed. I can imagine finding this pale, elfin form curled asleep amidst the ferns in my garden. But he only gets skinnier. Those who have visited him once in the hospital, the acquaintances and neighbors who have gone out of their way to meet my dying baby, now realize they may have to come again. I feel their horror and exhaustion. It's easy at first to respond to crisis, but this crisis is dragging on and on. No one we know has ever seen a baby like this before. He has shrunk by now from seven pounds to six or less. His hands are delicate twigs, bird bones, the skin on them almost translucent. The plates of his skull are prominent with sunken patches in between like the skin of a desiccated orange. The first time I feel his spine protruding, I think it must be something in his clothing, buttons, a zipper. Each vertebra protrudes. They're tiny. He's lying belly down on my chest in his pale blue terrycloth pajamas. I run my hand up and down his spine and imagine a lovely length of seed pearls. This is better than thinking of starvation.

Now we have different questions for the doctors than when we first arrived. Back then, we had the kinds of questions they could deal with – questions about cord blood gasses and EEGs – but now our questions are ones that never appeared in their textbooks. "What am I in for visually? How much worse will it get?" I ask every doctor I encounter, and every doctor looks bewildered.

"Be prepared for some weight loss…" one says.

"He will get thinner, perhaps," says another.

Vaguely, they deny the horror of his shrinking and move on. One day when I ask Dr. Z what we're in for, he suggests we seek "outside help" but as usual his euphemistic way of speaking confuses us. Does he mean help from a doctor other than him? Fortunately, David's stepmother is in the room to help. Carole assures Dr. Z that, seeing as both Larry and she are trained therapists, no one has forgotten about the benefits of therapy. Now Dr. Z misunderstands. He thinks she means that Larry and she will give David and me therapy. He launches into a story about the time his youngest child was a newborn and developed infant acne, and his wife freaked out and wouldn't let him diagnose it as something harmless. This is not the only time he's brought up his kids. Perhaps these stories are meant to give us hope for the future, but they don't. Or, rather, the only future I care about right now is Silvan's. Silvan has his own acne. There it is in the crease between lip and chin, a single bead, something to love, more proof that he's here, still alive, with the only pimple he will ever have.

When Dr. Z is done with his story, there is silence. "You know," he says, "this is really hard on the staff," as if we should take pity on him for burdening him with our son. When the silence remains, he licks his teeth. "But it's probably harder on the family…"

When he is gone, Carole tries to soothe me by saying, "What terrible bedside manners that man has."

BECAUSE WE'RE IN the hospital, because all of Silvan's life has been medicalized, we seem to think there should be an answer to this simple question: when? Not knowing feels like torture. But no doctor hazards a guess, not even based on statistics. Dr. Z won't even use the word "die." He says "pass" instead and the first time he uses it I think he's talking about passing gas.

How grateful we are, in contrast, for the nurses, for their honesty, their emotion.

The night nurse is particularly blunt. In future years, she predicts, we'll look back and say: *that was barbaric.* "We would never do this to an animal, we would never starve an animal, we euthanize our animals," she says. But is that true? I think of my cat Snowflake and how I failed her after college. She was my cat, it was my decision, my father said over the phone. However, surgery was expensive and the tumor likely to return. They were willing to pay for it, but she was twenty years old and a cat to whom surgery could not be explained, so euthanasia might be more compassionate.

And then, the clincher. "If you decide not to operate," my father said, "we will donate the cost of the operation to a human charity of your choice."

At that point, the washing machine in the background stopped. Both my parents were on the line, their voices made faint by the splitting of the call, but now my mother said she was going to put her receiver down to change the laundry. As soon as I heard that hollow thud, I saw my chance. In front of my mother, I was cautious, I was wary of her need to comfort, but alone with my father on the phone, I burst into tears because I wanted Snowflake to survive long enough for me to see her.

So I know it's complicated. I know that sometimes even for animals our emotions confuse our decisions. Because I cried, my parents operated on Snowflake, and I came home to see her, and a few weeks later she died anyway. We accidentally ran her over with the family car. There she lay, flopping in the driveway, dying in agony, after having survived a surgery so that I could pet her one last time.

After Snowflake died, I went down the hill to a cafe with paper and pen to write a letter to Maggy Brown. By then she was across the country in graduate school. With my innocence intact,

I wrote to her that at last I understood her grief. I had only an inkling of what I was talking about. Within a year, Mark had killed himself; within a year from Mark's death, my father died. Shortly after that, Maggy's father died; then a close friend from high school. Each time someone died, we called each other. No one else, we said, could understand.

And then I got the call about Maggy herself.

"I know I won't die yet," Maggy told me. We were in Baltimore together when she said this, passing a lush garden enclosed by a picket fence. "I know because I haven't learned the names for all those flowers yet." I had flown to her when I got the news. Her breast cancer was advanced, the treatments extreme, but she walked so fast, I couldn't keep up. Neither of us had hit thirty yet.

Maggy kept working, she won a prestigious grant from the French government, she moved to Paris; and she was flown back on a stretcher. The culture shock, the difficulties with the language weren't her fault. The cancer had spread to her brain. And here's where I failed her: though we'd grown proficient in talking about other people's deaths, we had no idea how to talk about our own. And yet even from a distance, I knew Maggy's death would come on Easter. In fact, I was so certain that even as I planned a brunch for that day I told David, "Maggy will die today. The call will come in the middle of the party, and I will excuse myself," which is exactly how it happened. The phone rang, I excused myself, and then I returned to the living room where I proposed a toast in honor of Maggy Brown.

FOR A DAY, David and I consider our options for Silvan as if his dying should be more in our control. Perhaps we should flee to a place where we can euthanize him. We know Oregon has some sort of legislation. Though the legislation has to do with consenting adults, perhaps it could be stretched to cover parents consenting on behalf of their child. We know that there always has to be someone to take the first public step for policy to change.

We know that, though Karen Ann Quinlan's parents were acting simply out of love for their child, their legal battle has made things better for us. Because of them, we were able to take that first step of removing Silvan's breathing tube. And because Quinlan survived the removal of her tube and went on to live for years in a coma before she finally died of pneumonia, some other family with some other comatose loved one must have fought for the right to remove artificial hydration and nutrition as well. Perhaps, we think, Silvan's life and death will have had greater purpose if his death allows future children to die more easily than he is.

For a day, I am fueled by rage again. I imagine us fleeing in a car, being stopped at the border, having to fight for the right to keep our son. I imagine our little family martyred. Again, I imagine some future book, this one fighting for the cause. But what cause is that? Silvan lies peacefully in my arms. A hundred years ago if he hadn't died at birth, if he hadn't died of his coma, he would have been one of those babies who mysteriously withered away. It would have been tragic even then, but at least there would've been a fund of common stories to help those parents through. Not knowing when he will die is horrible, but it is natural not to know. It is part of living. We are forced to ask ourselves whose suffering we care more about, our own or Silvan's.

The Future

"TAKE HIM HOME," THE NIGHT NURSE FINALLY SAYS ONE morning as she prepares to leave for the day. "At least do that." Though we've only ever met her a few times in passing, each time we do, she's blunt like this, this woman who spends her nights tending to our son. Silvan is almost a month old when she says it. She's not the first person to have asked why we hesitate. Friends have asked, doctors, nurses. But she's the only one who sounds certain this would be better.

At first, we resist even her bluntness. We remain afraid. We're afraid of not having institutional support, afraid of being the family that panics in the moment of death and calls 911 and has our baby revived yet again. David is afraid of having Silvan die at home and having us associate our house with his death. Though I'm not afraid of this, I also know there are no rituals around this kind of dying. Would people come and sit with us at home? Would we want them to come? How long are people willing to pay attention? Would we become isolated, alone with our dying baby? How long would we be able to sit with him alone? Would the demands of being at home distract us from the purity of this vigil?

For a few days, we carry on as usual. We scrub our hands and arms with antibacterial soap until our skin flakes; we listen to the parking attendant "pray for a miracle" for us each morning, and smile at the man at the front desk who easily spells my name now on the badges of our many visitors. Running into my mother around town, I see that she never bothers to take hers off. Sometimes I leave mine on, too, because it seems to explain what I'm going through. Wearing my badge, I hope to avoid the petty rage of pedestrians on the sidewalk who glare at me when I'm slowed by a sad thought against the usual flow of city life. It's a relief to get back to the hospital where everyone knows.

And yet, even in the hospital, the badge does not spare me awkwardness.

There is the nutritionist, a tall, handsome woman who breezes into the room one day and says, on her way to Silvan's chart, "Hello. I'm the nutritionist here."

"We're not doing a very good job of feeding him," I joke as she reads.

Spinning around, she leaves the room without another word.

There's the therapist who suggests that Silvan might benefit from massage, reads the chart, and also disappears.

And then there is Dr. Z with his constant refrain, "You will never regret this time with your son." This is about the only thing he says anymore. It seems almost a nervous tic, something he learned in med school, a useful protocol like checking blood pressure. He says it so often that one day I ask how he knows. "You may not understand now, but you will really know what I mean in the future, " he says.

At first I'm angry, I want to ask if he has done an objective study comparing the feelings of parents who starved their children to death with the feelings of parents whose children died in other ways. I want to ask how he knows about the future. I'm certain he's simply a coward. But at last his refrain begins to work on me. I think about "this time" with our son as something that will soon be gone. Until now, I've written in my diary with ambivalence. I've been suspicious of my penchant for thinking in terms of narrative. But now I realize what my mind is doing. If I understand my past by way of stories, I may also understand my future that way. I'm trying to find the story of Silvan that I'll someday tell myself. I want it to be a story I can bear to hear, a story of loving him well.

I START BY paying more attention to his bath schedule. What mother doesn't bathe her child? I bring him changes of clothes from home, washing my favorite outfits frequently. Then there's the problem of his hat. Though I keep bringing in new ones from home, hand-me-downs and gifts from his baby shower, at last his head shrinks so much that none of them will stay on, and I arrive one day to find that a nurse has made him a hat from the sleeve-end of a hospital onesie. Her effort is so loving, so attentive, and yet it depresses me, that he will die wearing this scrap made by a stranger. Late one afternoon, I announce, "I'm going to buy a hat for Silvan."

"You're crazy. You think you can handle being in a children's clothing store?" David asks.

"I'll be fine," I say, ruffled by his question, for am I not a good mother who can shop for her son? Don't I want someday to be able to say that I did this? And I am fine, and a good mother, except that I'm holding my breath, and the hats are refusing to be small enough, and the clothes hanging from the racks are swinging back and forth in playful mockery: *we are for children who are growing up*, they sing. I think I might faint. Finally, I have to ask the clerk if there are any hats that are really, really small because I have to get out of there fast. She pulls a range from a basket and they are so cute: little dogs, polka dots, a jungle scene. But which is right for Silvan? What is exactly him? I need a hat that will remind me of him forever and ever. A hat to die in. The hot spring sun blazes through the plate glass windows and the little hats keep coming; they are blurring, and in that blur is the only hat I will ever buy my son.

"Will any of these do?" the clerk asks.

I moan.

"They're certainly as small as the hats they give out at the hospital," she says.

"That's the problem. My son's in the hospital and needs an even smaller hat."

"How old is your son?" she asks.

I'm stunned. Have I just told her I have a son? I have a son! How amazing to be out in the world telling people that I have a son. I have a son, I repeat to myself, I have a son about whom people can ask this question. "Almost a month," I say. Can he really be so young?

"Don't worry, he'll be okay," she says.

"No," I wail. "No." And it is too awful, being in a children's store where everything is full of expectation. It is impossible. It is impossible that I am no longer an expectant mother. Who am I? Where is he?

Goodbye, Little Man

HE MUST COME HOME. HE MUST DIE AT HOME. IT IS AS if I'm bargaining with a genie who has given me three wishes. First, I asked for a baby but forgot to specify he should survive. Then I asked for him to die easily but forgot to say where. It is being in the hospital, I tell myself, it's being distracted from anything but Silvan that is making this so hard – as if death itself is not hard. *Good deaths happen at home*, I think. Even Mark knew this. Even Mark whose death I do not want to dwell on, whose death I've avoided telling until now, that final year, those final days. Halfway through college his misery had begun, his highs and lows. He'd managed to finish college, managed to find an apartment and get a job, but at twenty-five he'd moved back home, right before Snowflake died. For weeks we felt something coming as oppressive as a storm; for weeks he was vacillating ever higher and lower, hiding in the closet all one afternoon, insisting on another that I taste the orange juice he had made from the frozen concentrate in the freezer, insisting it was the best juice of his life while he paraded around in the vintage hats he kept bringing back from thrift stores. He lay in bed for hours, got up raring to help me clean our parents' house though I was the one paid to do it; I gave him the basement bathroom to clean and he was gone for hours, finally coming up in glowing triumph to lead me back down to admire what looked so much like the same old dingy bathroom with the beige tiles that I was surly in my thanks. He took me out for a beer saying it was my birthday, though it wasn't; and he spent most of the time raging around the bar, wooing strangers until the bouncer came over and shone a light in his eyes to see if he was on drugs. The next day, my mother called his therapist, begged her to do something, get him back on his meds, but the therapist, seduced by his charisma, said he was doing better than ever. He went to the neighbors' house and had them take his portrait in a crisp, maroon shirt. He spent that evening at home with me making beads out of clay. I saw later how he had been worrying in his diary for months about our feelings if he left us. I asked if he was suicidal and he said, "No."

It is awful, that my mother knew, that I knew, that still we failed to stop him. The strain was tremendous. I didn't want him to die. His suffering was temporary, it was cyclical. I wanted him to recover enough to see that life was worth living. But I felt trapped in the house with him, pressed up against his misery, or against his need for me to scale heights I could not achieve, and I writhed away from him. I spent whole evenings with him, trying to make him feel loved, but I also just wanted his need for me to stop so that, when he finally killed himself, it was not so much his escape from his suffering that pained me, but my own failure to ease that suffering in other ways.

On his last night, he asked if I was going to eat dinner with the rest of the family and I said, "No." I needed a break. No. My final word to him. The next morning, I found the garage door open, cold air pouring into the house, and I slammed it closed, not knowing. Did he leave it open on purpose? Was he hoping someone would follow him down into the lower basement and save him right up until that last second? How is it possible that it was only then, after he hanged himself, that I noticed the bathroom ceiling had been freed of mildew, that he had bleached away every last powdery flower?

NOW I NEED to learn from that final, ugly word "no" to end Silvan's story better. A nurse tells me that most babies die between four and six in the morning. Each morning, I wake up terrified. For weeks, we have considered spending nights on chairs by his bed, but with his heart still chugging along, unbearably strong, we have gone home to sleep, saving our strength. But it gets harder and harder to stay away. Not only am I afraid he'll die while I'm gone, but I suspect the only reason he needs the morphine the nurses have begun to give him is because we aren't there. Even though a nurse usually comes and offers to hold him when we leave for the night, I suspect he knows the difference. Always within an hour, the nurse reports that she has had to give him a dose.

I want to be his morphine, his solace to the end.

Still we hesitate.

It doesn't help that each time we bring up hospice, Dr. Z seems cagey. "It's very hard to get a slot with hospice," he says, "sometimes you have to wait weeks and by then..." On a Friday, he tells us we'll have to wait until Monday even to make a call. There is always a reason why we shouldn't even bother trying.

But if we don't have hospice to vouch for us, his death could get complicated. Without institutional support, we could be accused of murder. If he dies at home without hospice, 911 will have to sign the death certificate, and who knows how the paramedics will react. What will they think of us as parents? Anyone seeing Silvan for the first time would be horrified beyond belief. Though he is still beautiful to us, no one we know has ever seen a starving newborn quite like this. Not even in the news do babies starve like this, with enough medical care that their dying goes on and on.

At last we reach outside the hospital for help. We contact the nurse at the hospital where we'd considered transferring Silvan prior to the ethics committee meeting. She has a private line to the hospice organization that works with dying children. We call her on a Monday afternoon, she arranges to have a hospice nurse come and meet us at Silvan's bedside that evening, and we arrange with the hospice nurse to have Silvan discharged the next morning. In Silvan's chart, Dr. Z. takes note of this. He says we have "actually" contacted hospice without his help.

ON TUESDAY MORNING, I wake shaking. What if he has already died? What if he dies while we are on our way? What if I never get to bring him home? All the way to the hospital, I shake. In the elevator, I shake. As we sign in at the NICU and start to scrub our hands and arms, I'm still shaking. But at last we're in his room. And there he is, calmly sleeping in my mother's arms as he does each morning on her "shift."

And yet, I do not stop shaking.

Now I shake out of a different fear. Who am I to be responsible for this fragile being outside my womb? What if I hold him wrong? What if I drop him in the bath? What if he *dies*? I'm suddenly afraid to take him away from the safety of all this, his monitors, his nurses, all these people who know how to keep babies alive.

But the decision has been made: a nurse we've never met before is in charge of discharge. Efficiently, she shows us the bag of stuff the night nurse has prepared: diapers, saline solution and lube for his eyes, a thermometer, a stethoscope, his music box, and all his clothes. The night nurse has even changed him into a new undershirt beneath which I find no wires at all. All the monitoring is done. He is entirely free at last!

My shaking shifts again. Now I shake with eagerness to get away from all this, this artificial light and air, the beeping and whirring of machines, the constant press of strangers, to get away with him.

But, though he is free and mine, there is still more to do. Nurses come to say goodbye to him, all but Kerry who already said goodbye at the end of her shift the day before. She has danced a final dance with him, waltzing round the room to the music on his music box, both of them made ghastly and beautiful by impending death. He was her first terminal baby, and I have found her in tears more than once, and how I love her for it, that he is special to her. These other nurses are brave and beautiful, too. They spend as much time praising us and our decision as they do stroking Silvan's cheek and calling him "little man." We get his medications and instructions on how to administer them. He has morphine for pain, and lorazepam for anxiety, and phenobarbital for seizures, all given in teeny doses as needed, the only liquid he gets. We make sure we have our DNR form prominent so that he won't be resuscitated, whisked away, taken over by the state if we call 911 in a panic.

Finally, Dr. Z arrives.

"There is," he begins, "one little problem that has to be worked out before you leave."

Here it comes. He's going to throw up some roadblock and we will be trapped here forever, Silvan will die in this room.

But all he says is that we need to have a pediatrician lined up.

"Oh, yes, we have lined up… " we say and mention Dr. Z's boss.

He looks surprised. Once again we have worked behind his back.

Diplomatic David says, "It makes sense since he'll be on service after you."

Now we have one little problem for him. For weeks we've been pressing him on the question of organ donation. He thinks a newborn can donate corneas and heart valves. At least, before we leave, he can help us figure this one issue out.

He blinks his eyes, licks his lips. He takes up his soothing, hallmark tone of voice and says, "Your concern about organ donation is noble, but what you really need to be thinking about right now is yourselves. You need to be focusing on yourselves and your son." Behind him, a resident and a nurse nod somberly at the doctor's wisdom.

I feel slapped in the face. Is he suggesting I'm not focusing on my son? And what does he mean, I need to focus on myself? The gulf between us deepens. I feel like he's telling me the only way to survive this ordeal is to insulate myself from the world, whereas I feel that the only way I have been able to survive this ordeal – the only way I've been able to make this choice – is by seeing myself as part of a community. Because we're focused on more than ourselves, we can love Silvan enough to let him go.

We will have to do the footwork ourselves. When we get home, we'll call the organ donation number, and it'll be confirmed: corneas and heart valves. But then the woman on the other end of the line will ask his weight. Four pounds and falling. He'll be disqualified due to prematurity. But he is full-term, David will argue. Of course, this makes no sense to the woman. There is no space on any of her forms for term babies starved to death.

But I say nothing now and Dr. Z is safe in his element, floating in a river of clichés. "We do the best we can for our patients," he says for the millionth time, and, "You'll never regret the time you spend with your son."

Then he shakes my hand.

He shakes David's hand.

And then he leans down to where my mother sits holding Silvan. Already our comfortable leather glider has been given to another mother and my mother sits in a hard, wooden rocking chair. He leans down to where Silvan lies, eyes open and hands at his cheeks, and he shakes my mother's hand.

Then he leaves the room.

Dr. Z leaves without saying goodbye to Silvan!

I am furiously insulted. I am heartbroken. I'm not his patient. Silvan is! In my anger, I remember my father's doctor, who wouldn't tell my father if he was close to death. Instead, my father's doctor took the family out into the corridor a few days after Christmas and at our insistence told us, "soon he'll stop eating." He left us standing there, pondering this, wondering if it was necessary for my father to keep eating to stay alive, wondering how long that massive Christmas meal of duck à l'orange and plum pudding that we'd brought to his room, how long that champagne would last him, while my father lay in his bed yelling, "Tell that little schmuck to come in here and face me like a man."

WE STILL HAVE a good hour of hanging around, waiting for paperwork to be sorted, medication to arrive, but at last we're in the hallway at our locker for the last time, retrieving the boom box, the picnic blanket, and here comes Dr. Z, going by on rounds with his residents around him like a hen with her skittish chicks, and I think perhaps he will redeem himself in the final hour. Indeed, he does not pass us up. But then he starts to talk again, the same clichés. I keep looking down at Silvan to give him a clue that he should pay attention to his patient more than to us, but he doesn't catch on. He's all big smiles and nods of his head, clearly relieved, almost ecstatic to be rid of us, and then he's on his way again, to babies whose lives he can save.

But one resident lingers. Here it is: is she still "here" for our family as she had told us on the first day of this ordeal?

"I just want you to know," she says, twisting her fingers in the beads of the necklace that holds her hospital I.D., "that I've learned a tremendous amount from you, both professionally and personally, and I will never forget it."

Then she leans towards Silvan. Her eyes fill with tears. With the backs of two fingers, she strokes his cheek, over and over. "'Bye, little Silvan; goodbye, little man." Then, with a nod, she is off, following the others.

First Night

FIRST THING I DO AT HOME IS PUT SILVAN DOWN IN A swing seat. No need to buckle him in, though, since my boy never moves. It is the 27th of May; he is exactly one month old. On the way home from the hospital, I held him in my arms in the front seat while David drove. Damned if I was going to make him suffer a car seat. I kept up a one-sided conversation in the car, remarking on every change to Silvan's face. He seemed to be listening to this car ride. Whenever a particularly loud, deep engine passed us, his body stiffened slightly and he'd move his eyes side to side as if excited or alarmed.

"Like all little boys, Silvan is interested in cars," I told David.

At home, after putting him down in his little jungle swing seat, I move a stack of papers. Again, he moves his eyes from side to side, listening. For the next few days, each time I fiddle with paper, he wakes up and listens. But when I bring him to hear the kettle whistle, there is no response; and, even worse, there is no response when David plays him "Twinkle, Twinkle Little Star" on the saxophone. After a few days, he stops responding even to the paper crinkling. But he does still wake up when David drops something on the kitchen floor. David's friend Michael is over once when Silvan is awakened by lunchtime preparations. Michael is in residency, training to be an obstetrician, and he kneels beside Silvan's rocking chair and moves his finger from side to side in front of Silvan's eyes. Though we have told him the diagnosis and prognosis, Michael wants to test this for himself.

"He *can* see," he says. "Look, he's tracking my finger."

But no, we say. That's just what he does, moves his eyes side to side. Now do something different, we say, stay in one place awhile.

Sure enough, Silvan's eyes continue moving side to side.

The thing is, though we can pass along to others a diagnosis and prognosis in which we're by now well-schooled, we ourselves are still tempted to search for signs of health. Maybe he no longer reacts to paper crinkling not because he's getting weaker, but because he's figured it out, the sound no longer interests him. Maybe he doesn't want to play Michael's finger game.

PUTTING SILVAN DOWN in that rocking swing is a sweet relief because it's normal. Until now, whenever I was with Silvan, I was holding him. While we were in the hospital together, he was a patient I tended but now he can be near me while I do normal, parent-as-person things: cook dinner, make a bed. We are home at last with our one-month-old.

The first night, we make the bed carefully. Margie has lent us her solution to sleeping with a baby without fear of crushing him. It is an odd, inflatable wedge we place between our two pillows so his head is raised higher than our pillows but his body can be partially tucked beneath our blankets. He's so cold all the time, he needs the warmth of our blankets. Afraid that he will be dead before I wake again, I place my head directly next to his and put his little hand in mine.

"I'm right here," I tell him in the dark. Without the monitor to plug him into, I am his new, human monitor.

Two hours later, at the time he always woke me in utero, at the time he always woke in the hospital, he wakes me with his new, little cry. It is, as David calls it, his creaky door cry. He makes this noise at most two or three times a day.

"I'm right here," I tell him. How much closer can I get? Yet, when I do not respond with more than that, he actually cries a sweet, dove cry that I have never heard before.

This wakes David who tries to soothe Silvan, too. We sing, touch him, rock him in his little bed. Nothing works. I will have to get out of bed with him and give him morphine just like the nurses did. And yet, in the living room, in my arms, he's instantly calm. It's me he wants, it seems, my full attention. Or perhaps I'm projecting. I want to feel his need. But not wanting to risk him crying as soon as I get back in bed, I lie on the sofa. I remove the back cushions and curl with him between me and the sofa back. For a moment, he paws my chest like a kitten, pushing me from him, then settles. I place his little, bumpy skull in the palm of my hand. When David wakes us at dawn, Silvan's little head is still cupped in my palm.

MARGIE'S HUSBAND GAVIN tries to think of something to occupy us now that we're home all the time with our child, but I tell him I'm as busy as any parent with a newborn just getting things done. Of course, things for Silvan are not ordinary. There's his medicine – for after that first night's triumph, I find my arms don't always stop his cry. With the hospice nurse, we work out a morphine schedule to minimize his suffering. He can barely choke down his dose – I hear it chugging through him as if he's hollow inside – and I call his doctor and beg for something more concentrated, so a drop will be enough. We also give him pheno-barbital after I spot little hand seizures. The phenobarbital seems too much for him too, both in size and effect; he lies there in a glazed daze. I call his doctor again to describe the seizures I am trying to treat, I mention how the seizures seem to make him anxious more than pain him. Instinctively, I ask if I could treat him with the anti-anxiety medication lorazepam instead, and the doctor agrees. When the lorazepam also stops the seizures, I feel triumphant as a mother, as if I've guessed just what food my picky baby will eat. In addition to this, there are things like his diaper to check. The first week home there's still a little pee, like saffron, clinging to his penis. And there are baths to give. There's

Vaseline to apply to his drying lips, no longer plump and magenta like his father's but pale pink and thin, but still exquisitely shaped, and the Vaseline makes them look alive again, though the reason we apply it is for his comfort. Same with lube for his eyes – he blinks so infrequently they get dry. We apply lube so earnestly that one day we realize the little cracks appearing on his eyeballs are actually fluff and a tiny strand of hair that have stuck in the lube, so we have to flush his eyes with saline. We flush them so well the first time that the space behind his eyeballs fills with saline; we have to squeeze it out like tears.

But these things do not perturb him. In fact, he seems particularly calm as David ministers to him. Because it is David who does the nursing. Caring for his son in this way is perfect for David. As he carefully drops the saline into Silvan's eyes, everything in the room becomes still and calm. Father and son. I watch with amazement that tenderness, and understand Silvan's calmness in those hands.

Once, my belly big with Silvan a few months back, I'd complained to David that he wasn't verbally loving enough, and he'd said he preferred to show his love in action. Weeks from now, he'll show me what he means again. I will step on something small that lodges in my foot. Night after night, David will hold my foot in his steady, warm hands and search for this tiny, invisible source of my pain.

TWO DAYS AFTER we bring Silvan home, I call the NICU to let Kerry know how Silvan is doing at home. She asked me to do this. Everyone expects he will die soon, but still Kerry wants to know how he's doing while he remains alive. With disappointment, I realize as I dial that I have missed the shift of the husky-voiced Shelley by a few minutes. I'm yearning for her soothing tone. The afternoon receptionist is quite the opposite, harried, unfriendly.

"Kerry?" she says in a cold voice. "There's no one here by that name."

"I'm sorry," I say, "I mean Nurse Kerry. Nurse Kerry

Campbell." I am strangely near tears, as unsure of my place in her world as a runaway child.

"There's no one here by that name," she repeats.

"Yes, there is." I try another tack. "This is Baby Boy Wesolowska's mother."

"That baby was sent home," she says.

"I know, I'm his *mother*. He's home with *me*," I say. "But Kerry has been his nurse for the last month."

"On this shift?"

"Yes."

"I've been here twenty-five years and we don't have a nurse by that name."

When I insist, she says she'll go ask the charge nurse.

A few minutes later, she returns, sounding irritated. "She's a *new* nurse. I'll transfer you." I almost want her to continue insisting there's no Kerry. For if there is no Kerry, perhaps the world Kerry belongs to no longer exists. Perhaps it was a world made up by a genie who whisked me there for a while before returning me to real life. Perhaps the whole thing was a bad dream. Perhaps I am about to wake up.

Circuit Tester

"OH MY GOD, I THINK HE HAS NECROSIS," DAVID SAYS. We stare in horror. Now that he can't possibly get any skinnier is Silvan's skin dying? We run our fingers gently along the odd pattern of depressions on his thigh. The days creep by even more slowly now than in the hospital, immersed as they are in such horrifying detail, the unknown end always receding before us. He is thirty-three days old, then thirty-four. We wait eagerly for the next home visit from the hospice nurse. When she arrives, we place him on the sofa beside her and take off his diaper to show her the necrosis. "Hmmm," she says, leaning in close and running her own fingers across it. "I'd say this is where the diaper was a little too tight." She's not trying to make us feel foolish, but we do.

Another time, he smells funny. The smell seems to come from his mouth but it is strong enough to mask the sweet loam of his head, the powdery perfume of his neck.

Is this the death smell one nurse told us about?

I'm sure it is; and I am heartbroken.

But sniffing again, I find it more medicinal than deathly, and I remember how his tongue had turned blue from morphine in the hospital. No one had seemed particularly concerned. Still, we open his mouth wide to check. My god, not only is his tongue bright blue, but he has stalagmites and stalactites of yellow goo, an accretion of medicine, lifting from his tongue and falling from the roof of his mouth.

Baby. Is it unpleasant for you in there?

We are now on a mission to clean his mouth of goo. There's nothing in any of our baby books about this. After trying a wet Q-tip and a rubber spoon to no effect, we try some mouthwash sponges we were given at the hospital, little pink lollipops of foam on sticks. I cannot watch as David forces the sponge into Silvan's mouth.

"Silvan doesn't like this one bit," David says.

I'm relieved. If Silvan can still protest what he does not like, then in his usual quietness he must not be suffering.

EACH AFTERNOON WE have a variety of visitors, family, friends, neighbors. We sit in the backyard in the swinging seat I bought when I imagined being a nursing mother this first summer of his life. We pass him around and chat and enjoy the flowers and the sun. It is the end of May, the unruly jasmine on the fence is bursting with sweet smells despite our singular focus on the sweetness of Silvan. He's been home now for only four days, though each day feels as long as a week.

In that time, the flow of love from others has not stopped. But, with other people around, the horror of Silvan's dying is more obvious to us. He is yellow as a cheese rind, he looks as fleshless as a skull. His mouth has started hanging open. His eyes are huge and round. They are still beautiful, brown and blue and green, with thick, dark lashes around them, and pupils that respond – how proud we are of those responsive pupils! – but he can longer close them. He is too weak, or his eyelids have shrunk, or he's forgotten about blinking. Day and night he stares without a blink. He is thirty-four days old, then thirty-five, always staring out.

People hold him still but now there is more sadness, more exhaustion. One day my mother even says he looks pathetic. My mother, who has held him more than anyone, for hours and hours and hours, has said he looks pathetic. I am crushed. How can she call him pathetic when he is doing the most amazing thing, staying alive, day after day? I don't want people around who think he looks pathetic. I want everyone to adore him as much as I do.

"Day and night?" Claudia asks us to clarify. I've just explained about Silvan's eyes remaining open all the time. Claudia visits now that we are out of hospital, but the difficulties continue. She clutches an open-eyed Silvan to her pregnant belly. "It doesn't matter, it doesn't matter," she repeats in a mysterious chant. She paces our house late one afternoon, going from window to window, as if looking for a place to escape. Perhaps she disagrees with our choice, but she hasn't said as much. The closest she's come is saying, "This would be a lot harder if you already had children and knew how much you were going to lose." It pains me that she doesn't think I'm suffering as much as she would. It pains me that she has no idea how much I love him. It pains me that she hasn't yet realized *he is my child*.

"So if his eyes are always open how can you tell if he's asleep?" she asks now.

"We know," David says, "because when he's awake, his eyes move from side to side."

"But how can you tell he's not in pain?" In the same way, Brian had grilled us, wanting to know how we had chosen this method of death over something "more natural" like death by pneumonia as if death by pneumonia were more compassionate, as if we have a rational answer, as if we have proof or comparisons to rely on. As if we're not suffering through our choice because we feel it is right.

"He makes a noise when he's uncomfortable," David says.

"And when he's not awake, how can you tell he's still alive?" she goes on.

"Well," I say, unsure how to answer this. "He breathes…"

"Oh, yes, breathing," Claudia says, visibly embarrassed. She still clutches Silvan but thoughtlessly, like a football, as if she has forgotten he is no ordinary baby but one who is dying and must be held with that thought in mind. I ask her to give him back. She refuses. For a second, I take pity on her, whatever

terror holds her in its grip. I try to let her into my world. I say,
"It's true, sometimes you can't tell, through all the blankets. That's
why my sister was so happy to discover a special button. We call
it the circuit tester button."

I reach towards Silvan to demonstrate. Sure enough, it
works.

David and I laugh. When you touch Silvan's nose, he blinks;
or tries to. How cute he is. How sweet that little blink. How sad
that his blink is almost all we have.

Claudia does not laugh. She looks horrified.

Again, I ask her to give Silvan back. We are standing by
a window and there's coldness radiating from it, the fog of early
summer blowing in from the ocean. She looks as if she might
leap out that window with him.

I'm afraid he's getting cold.

She hesitates.

I insist.

Miracle Baby

PERHAPS HE IS MY MIRACLE BABY, AFTER ALL. PERHAPS he will never die. Thirty-five days old, thirty-six. I'm lying with him on the sofa, both of us under a blanket. It's evening and everyone has gone home and Silvan's mouth snaps shut. As if he's determined to be cutest for us alone. He pouts, and I coo with pleasure.

Some nights I read with him in my arms. Another night we watch a movie. It's almost normal. I stroke his head over and over until, engrossed in a silly romantic comedy ending in marriage, I forget there's anything wrong: I have become what I expected, mother and child, and my grief when I realize the deception of this image is explosive.

Later in bed, I lie in the dark trying to figure out if he's gasping. I have to keep waking David to turn on the light. I panic about the room not being warm enough, insist on turning on the heat, even though it's already June.

His little hands. Cold and floppy.

The next morning, I wake up sure he's dead from the feel of that hand. But he is very gently breathing, cupped between my arm and my side, and when I let go of his other hand, the one that has been engulfed in mine all night, it stays warm, warm, warm. Thank god. More time.

IT BECOMES HARDER and harder to turn out the light each night. Thirty-five days old, thirty-six. Time has stopped, time is repeating; but what if he dies before we wake? What will happen to time then? As David goes through his bedtime rituals, I lie beside Silvan and admire him. Although he's pale as wax and his cheekbones and eye sockets are too prominent, he still has a beautiful profile. He still has the profile of the little boy he should have been. From the side, I can admire the shape of that face, the sloping forehead, the button nose. When David finally gets in bed, we take turns kissing Silvan. Always I have to give the last kiss.

With his first cry later in the night, I'm relieved. I've just been wrenched from a dream in which he is ill and dying and my first thought is "Thank god that was a dream." By then I am fully awake, comforting my son, relieved he's alive and also horrified to find the dream is true.

THE SKIN ON his forehead is hard and dry as cheap suede by now and I have to be careful with his bones, his joints; there are positions in which he doesn't like to lie. He's no longer a malleable bundle. He doesn't like to go on walks in my arms. When I stroke his back, each vertebra protrudes and it is a relief to reach his buttocks which, along with the soles of his feet, are the only part of him with enough fleshiness still to feel soft as a baby's feet should. Those soles get me every time, soft and pale with a crease down the middle, those peas for toes.

One morning, I ask David to take a photograph so I can see the sweetness I'm feeling as we lie together in bed. I can feel Silvan's eyelashes moving on the skin of my neck, the butterfly kisses I have not felt since my father used to give them, telling me to stay still and quiet, to pay attention to this tiny gift of his eyelashes moving on my cheek. But the outside view of this moment tells a different story—there I lie, exhausted, with a creature on me, his arms as thin as sticks, his lips open against my chest as if making one last attempt to feed. It is the only photo that truly horrifies me. It is an image I would prefer not to have created with words. But I must be honest. In a different world, loving him enough to let him die could have been less awful.

"WHAT WOULD YOU say if I gave him a fatal dose?" David finally asks. He's hitting a wall. Morphine was held out to us as the panacea, and yet now that we're here, we're told that people get used to morphine, that a baby especially can metabolize and live for a long time on increasing doses. Thirty-five days old, thirty-six; perhaps he will always be alive.

"Is there even such a thing?" I say.

David doesn't know and the question is stalled for another day.

Each day it seems Silvan can't possibly survive another; and then it is morning again, and David is having thoughts of morphine. I worry my husband will lose his sanity if he can't give his son a fatal dose. And I'm afraid he will lose his sanity if he does. If our suffering is necessary proof that we have made this choice out of love, then we are proving our love in spades. This is not the slippery slope towards callous euthanasia; this is the steep climb, I think, towards something more selfless and noble. But finally, I have to ask David to stop talking about it. I tell him I can't risk having him accused of murder. I can't risk him *feeling* like a murderer. This is the law, whether we like it or not. We don't have this choice. Besides, we are nearer to the end than the beginning now. Can't he wait?

And maybe it's easier this way, to forbid him.

Forbidden, David admits he couldn't have done it.

AND THEN IT finally comes. In the middle of the night, in the middle of our bed. We think our baby is gasping his last. The sound wakes us from heavy sleep to horror. David turns on the light. I hold Silvan while David fills the dropper with morphine.

This will be, we are sure, his final dose, the dose given to relieve "agonal" breathing, the dose that relieves the pain of death. And yet I'm sick from having been jarred from sleep. My arms feel too weak to hold my baby. David thinks we should each administer half the dose so that neither of us will feel responsible. He goes first. We're both sobbing. The bed sheets are in a tangle beneath us and it is hard to sit up. I don't want to say goodbye to him like this, half asleep, in the mess of our bed. David says we should sing. He breaks into our song:

> You are my Silvan, my only Silvan
> You make me happy when skies are blue
> You'll never know, dear...

I try to join in but my throat closes and still David goes on –

> I dreamed I held you in my arms

– but I am so sleepy, I want nothing more than to flop down and maybe I can, because Silvan seems to have recovered.

We stare in disbelief. Yes, his breathing has become soft and easy again. In a flash, the terror that he would die is replaced with the horror that he has not, which is replaced with relief that he's still with us.

"YOU DID THE right thing," the hospice nurse tells us the next morning.

"But why did he recover?"

She looks surprised. "The morphine just relaxes his breathing so he's not uncomfortable. It will only help him die if he's already dying."

All that next day, we stay home alone with him, but there is no change, no more scares. At last, needing relief, I call my mother. She's at our house within ten minutes. As David and I walk around the neighborhood together without Silvan, I am at peace knowing he's in his grandmother's arms and that within a short while, he'll be back in mine, and that we may go on and on like this forever. Just like with Mark in those last weeks of his life, it's impossible to believe that Silvan will ever really give up. After all, I'm getting used to him, to the strain of loving him to death.

Joy

"HIS SYSTEM IS STARTING TO SHUT DOWN," THE HOSPICE nurse finally tells us. It is early June; Silvan has been alive for thirty-eight days. We have been waiting since April, and yet now that I'm told his end is near, I no longer believe it. The phrase itself repels me. "Shutting down." I remember seeing his heart in my first ultrasound. To my surprise, the sight made me cry. There it was, this new life, this second heart beating right inside me. The last thing in the world I want is for that system to shut down. Shutting down means we are past the point of no return. *His beautiful kidneys, his exquisite liver, his heart. They are being ruined. They are betraying him. We have betrayed him. Soon he won't even be able to take another breath. Don't leave me Silvan. Please don't leave me. I didn't mean it. I'm sorry. I'm so very sorry.* And so it passes through my mind and yet, here I am, still sitting in my armchair holding my dying son and nodding at the hospice nurse.

But she can tell. "What will make it okay for him to go?" she asks gently, turning, for the first time, all of her attention on us.

"I just need him to die in my arms." As I say it, I feel all the desperation in my voice of someone making a final wish. I am bargaining with the genie again. If I'm to have a baby who will die, then *please* just let him die in my arms. After having come so far with him, how can I not be granted this one, tiny wish that he not be alone at the end?

"Do you understand it may not happen the way you need it to happen?" she asks.

Of course, this is death we're talking about. I nod. Just as I
could not control his conception, his birth, I know I cannot
control his death. And yet, I am pleading. I cannot imagine any
other end but in my arms.

His temperature is way down, she reports. He has not peed
in days and days. His heart is beating slower and his breathing
is irregular. "His system is definitely shutting down," she says,
"but as to time, it could be today, it could be a couple of days."

"Could it be another week?" I ask.

"No, no, I don't think another week," she says.

She doesn't *think* so? No one has ever thought it could be
another week. But if it is another week, does that perhaps mean
he will go on forever?

He takes three breaths. We wait. He takes another breath.

DAVID SETS UP the little inflatable mattress on the table next
to my plate. We're eating chicken with Gavin whom we'd called
that morning and begged to come soon, to come today. Gavin
hasn't been by since we brought Silvan home and there isn't much
time left. Every so often, I turn from the lunchtime conversation
and check on Silvan. He's so calm, his brow unwrinkled. I run my
finger across that brow and the day seems perfect: good company, good food, my baby there within reach. How glad I am to
have that balance; everyone at peace. There is a veil of clouds
on the sky, a golden warmth to the day, that pleases Gavin and me.
We talk about favorite temperatures and humidities and the
simplicity of our pleasure is satisfying.

Then, as lunch ends, Silvan gives his little, creaky door cry,
not much, but with a baby who asks for so little, we jump for his
slightest wish.

I pick him up and hold him in the kitchen while David does
the dishes. Then we go into the living room. I sit, still holding
Silvan. Gavin has just told us he's been feeling down for months,
that this is why we haven't seen more of him. He's struggling as
a stay-at-home dad. Then he apologizes for having a complaint

so petty in comparison to ours and I love him for it. Still, I start to have that feeling that I need to be alone with Silvan. I think perhaps I'll excuse myself to give him a bath. This, I'm sure, will be the last bath. I am eager for one last bath. I need to see his body in all its naked glory. But first, it is time for his scheduled medication – he is so calm, it hardly seems necessary, but I don't want him slipping into pain. I sit him up.

David gives him his doses. I wait for Silvan to swallow, then lower him to the crook of my arm. But something gurgles, like he is snoring with every exhalation.

"What's that noise?" I ask.

"Oh, no," David says, "He's got medication in the back of his throat."

He takes Silvan from me. He holds him face downward but nothing comes out and the snores still come.

"Do you think it's the death rattle?"

David shakes his head. He's sure it's the medication. He takes Silvan and rotates him side to side. Then he gently turns him upside down. For a moment, that's okay with Silvan. Then, as the skin of his face puckers around his chin and grows pink, he reacts, gives his squawk.

"Give him back," I say.

David gives him back.

I soothe Silvan with a mock criticism of the beating he's taken at the hands of his father, but David seems to have fixed the problem. The rattle is gone. Silvan has resumed his slow, calm breathing.

We continue our conversation and then, a pleasant ten or fifteen minutes later, while Gavin is talking, or David is talking, or somewhere in between, there is no breath. How do I feel no breath? And how long ago was breath? The bundle of Silvan feels different. Heavier, more still. I watch his nostrils. I will not alarm David unnecessarily. I watch. No breath comes. No breath comes. The men continue talking about something I cannot hear. I put my fingers to his neck. I've never felt for his pulse this way before. I feel no pulse. But I've never felt for it before. Maybe I just don't know how. So I watch his nostrils again. Still no breath. I put my fingers to his neck. Still no pulse. Then David notices something different in me.

"What's wrong?" he asks.

"I can't feel a pulse."

Gavin grabs his jacket, I think I nod at him as he slides from our house.

David goes for the stethoscope. He listens to Silvan's chest.

"Is there a heartbeat?" I ask.

"I don't think there is one," he says.

So we sit there. *David doesn't know either*, I think. After a while, I say, "So do you think he's still alive?"

"No. There's no heartbeat," he says.

"Oh my god. I was sitting here thinking you didn't know, because you said you didn't *think* there was a heartbeat."

"I'm sorry, I think he's dead, " David says. "I mean, he *is* dead."

I SIT WITH my son. He is warm and still and calm.

Both my sister and David's sister are expected for visits shortly so I ask David to call them and tell them not to come.

He isn't ready yet to say Silvan is dead and so he says, "Hold off on coming. Silvan's having a hard time." Then I realize that my sister may go out for the evening instead of coming here and that my mother will be alone when we call back. So I have David call with the truth. And he calls his sister back too but his sister has already left work so he has to leave a message on her home phone, then he calls his dad with the news, and his mom who keeps asking questions even though he says he has to go, then the hospice worker. The disparity is tremendous: mother sitting calmly with her child while father does, does, does. But, after the frenzy of the phone calls, it is David's turn to sit with his son, while I get up to stretch my arms.

I go to the bathroom, although I don't really need to pee,

but somehow going pee seems a way to keep going, to acknowledge that I'm still here after all.

The hospice nurse will arrive in an hour to "pronounce" Silvan, meaning to pronounce him dead, a bureaucratic necessity to guard against burying people alive, I guess. If hospice doesn't do it, we'll have to call 911.

That means for one hour more he is not quite dead.

I take him back from David. The bundle is still warm and I can feel still like a mother with her babe in arms. But he is getting heavier.

The hospice nurse told us from the beginning that one of the things she could do for us at the end is help bathe him. But I'd hoped to do it on my own.

Now David asks if he can help.

We fill the bath, as usual, in the sink. As always, we test the water, making it nice and warm. We set up the soft changing table on the counter, get two clean towels, including one with a hood so his head won't get cold as we're drying him. Then I carry him into the kitchen and put him on the changing table. Undressing him is fine until I get to the diaper and there, after days of no pee, after a month of no poop, is a yellow stain and a tarry plug. I freak.

I say, "I can't do this." I am thinking of the rest of my dead.

But there is David, he keeps us going. He disposes of the diaper and lifts Silvan's body – now strangely heavy – into the water where his limbs loosen and float.

The sun comes slanting into the kitchen, lighting up the yellow table and walls. I start with his head, just as you are supposed to do with babies, lifting the clean cloth to his eyes. As the water runs into his eyes, the lube and dust coating them melt away and we see them – that green and blue and brown fringed with lustrous lashes. We wash his lips, so full once, now like exquisite etchings, and behind his downy ears; we wash the hair on his head which, in the bright kitchen, shows itself to have hints of red in its brown. We wash his bony chest, the tiny hollows of his armpits, those delicate fingers. We run the washcloth down the laddered bones of his back, and over his still-soft buttocks and down his long legs to his feet, those tender soles.

Once we have dried him thoroughly, I go for the receiving blanket. None of this has been consciously planned, because I knew I could not predict how I would feel at this moment, but as I go through the motions, I have a sense of having already rehearsed.

He lies on his changing table with his limbs fully extended, something he never did in life. With the calmness of someone who lives both inside and outside of herself, I have David take a picture of Silvan's skeletal corpse in case we want to show people in the future what a death like this looks like. As if the horror of this picture could possibly convey the depths of what the three of us have gone through.

Then, because Silvan in life liked to be curled up, I bend his knees towards his chest and lower his elbows towards his knees, afraid if I don't do it now, he will become stiff in his vulnerable, unnatural pose.

David insists on swabbing the interior of Silvan's mouth one last time while I hover, exhorting him not to spend too long at it, not wanting Silvan's mouth to stay open forever.

Then I swaddle him more carefully than I ever have. The receiving blanket is particularly nice, a thick white cotton with green stitching around the borders. David teases me for whatever it is that makes women treat fabric designed for babies almost as tenderly as they treat babies themselves.

But there is no denying that Silvan, carefully bundled in bright white, is angelic.

"Should we close his eyes?" David asks then.

"No," I say, "I'm used to them open by now."

FOR SOME REASON, we decide to take him into the backyard, as if this too is tradition, or part of our plan.

There, in the sunlight, he is even more magnificent, the

color of his eyes and hair breathtaking against the luminescent white of his skin. Again, we take pictures and it no longer feels like cold reportage, but something familiar, something people used to do routinely, recording their loved ones after death, proof that they have gone.

But time is passing. The hospice nurse will be here by six o'clock.

We bring him inside where I lay him again on his little bed still on the dining room table where, just a short while before, he had lain beside me during lunch.

It's time for tea.

A FEW MINUTES later, cup of tea in hand, I stand looking down at my peaceful son, and it seems suddenly a shame not to offer this vision to others.

My sister answers the phone. I can feel my mother suffer-ing in the background and I ask for her immediately. "Oh, yes, yes," she says to my offer to come and see Silvan and, "Can your sister come too?"

"Yes, but hurry, hurry," I say because they must see him before the hospice nurse arrives, while he is still in that in-between place, while his soul still seems to hover nearby. For that is the sense I have. That his soul is there making me ... elated, almost. As if his death like this, in my arms, in the middle of the afternoon, is his gift to me.

My mother and Katya arrive, Katya with the little some-thing she'd promised to bring him today: a new hat. It is just the sort of hat I'd looked for on my hat hunt earlier, a stocking cap with blue and white stripes. She asks if she could at least put it on. It's enormous on him. We laugh at how silly he looks. Then I take it off because I'm not letting Silvan leave us with the indignity of clothes too big for him. His hair has been tousled by the hat and Katya tries to smooth it, running her hands against the grain.

When she is done, I smooth it my way. We laugh again.

In all of this, my mother remains somber.

Katya grasps one of his knees.

EVERYONE BUT US is gone now. It is six o'clock and the hospice nurse arrives. She's her usual self and she speaks to Silvan in her usual way. She opens his swaddling blanket saying, "I'm just going to take a little listen here; there you go, the stethoscope is a little cold." Then she says to us, "Listen to me, I still talk to him like he's alive," which makes sense to us. And then she says to him, "Okay, all done, I'm going to wrap you up now."

She sits down to fill out a form which, I presume, will pronounce him dead, although it does cross my mind, the way she continues talking to him, that there might be a faint heartbeat, that it's a good thing we treated him so tenderly in his bath, always keeping his head above water, his neck supported, his bony backside from weighing too heavily on the roughness at the bottom of the tub.

She goes with David into the kitchen so he can witness her disposing of our extra narcotics, and he makes jokes about how he should have filled the bottles with replacement liquid and spirited the morphine away for himself. Life is going on, people going about their business, with Silvan lying here. The magic is dissipating. It's time to call the mortuary, but David's dad hasn't arrived yet and his sister hasn't decided what to do, and my brother is unreachable. I'm the one plying the phones now, postponing calling the mortuary, postponing the time when his body, which still gives me joy to see, will be truly gone.

But then, when David's Dad arrives – he's made it across the bridge in record time, a blessing – I see the truth.

Silvan's pupils are still magnificent – "Isn't he beautiful?" I say to my father-in-law, and, "Doesn't he look peaceful?" – but the whites are changing, turning the darkening color between yolk and white in an old hard-boiled egg.

"ARE YOU READY for me to be here?" the undertaker asks when he arrives at eight o'clock.

I've spent the last half an hour after hospice left simply sitting and admiring Silvan's face, to memorize each detail, to suck it through my eyes until it's so imprinted on my brain that I'm guaranteed the ability to recall it at will from now until eternity.

David says yes and lets him in where he asks me the same question.

I assume there will be paperwork to do, information to convey, but here it is: he has come for my baby. The undertaker is an obese man missing one arm from the elbow down. Held in the armpit of that truncated arm is a large square of folded plastic. My eyes keep wandering to the plastic and I feel bad, not wanting him to think it's his arm I'm looking at, not wanting him to know that in my grief, it seems too cruel for a perfect baby to die while a marred human being like him goes on. Finally, I ask him about the plastic under his arm. "Is that for carrying him out?"

"Yes, he will go out of here entirely covered," he says.

Having been warned by hospice about this, we have come up with a plan to avoid seeing Silvan carried away from us covered. I tell the undertaker my plan and he agrees readily and removes himself to the sidewalk by his van.

When we're alone again, I unwrap Silvan one last time and kiss his skinny chest between protruding nipples and then the sole of each foot. David does the same. Then, carefully, carefully, I wrap him again in his receiving blanket, now a departure blanket, the rest of him as perfectly naked as the day he was born.

We go to the front door and David opens it and I carry Silvan out onto the porch and carefully place him on the marble-topped table beneath the potted fig tree. The undertaker has left his square of folded plastic there. The temperature on the porch is pleasant, there seems something symbolic about the fig tree.

David says goodbye first. I insist. It feels impossible for me not to have the last goodbye.

But here it is. This is it.

As I lean over Silvan, I notice the giant trees in the yard two doors down, the giant trees full of birds that have awakened me each morning since Silvan's birth with their joyous, springtime greeting of the dawn. Those trees have caught in their upper limbs the last of the sunlight; from a crack beneath encroaching fog, long arms of gold weave through the green. The beauty gives me – for lack of any better word – hope. I lean close to Silvan and his open eyes. I kiss his forehead, his nose, his lips.

"Goodbye, Little Monkey," I say.

But that isn't right. How can that be the last thing I say to him? He isn't a monkey at all. He is a baby boy. My baby boy. My Silvan. What is the last thing he needs to hear from me before he goes out on his own? How is he to know, young as he is, who he is and by whom he is loved?

But I have to be fast about this. The undertaker is down there by his van. I've seen him through the window, pacing, and although he has told us to take all the time we want, he can't mean forever, can he? And besides, what if a neighbor sees me with my baby and comes to visit now? Or what if a passing stranger sees me and is horrified? The street is empty, darkening, everyone but us chased away.

"I love you, Silvan," I say and then, before I can ruin it with anything else and have to start again, I turn swiftly, carrying David swiftly with me, swiftly crossing the threshold back into our house, letting the screen door bang, leaving Silvan's body out there in the glorious evening air – the hardest thing I've ever done – because it is his body now, and no longer part of mine.

I BOLT UPRIGHT in the middle of the night. Something is missing. I search in the dark for something on the bed, something on the chair with my books, over there by the bassinet piled high with blankets.

"What's wrong?" David asks.

Then I realize what's missing. "Where is Silvan?"

"Silvan's gone." David says.

He thinks I've gone nuts, but he says nothing. We go back to sleep.

Minutes later, David wakes looking for Silvan. Then he, too, remembers.

HIS LITTLE UNDERSHIRT retains his smell. Once a day, I allow myself to dig it out of the laundry basket and inhale deeply.

On the third day, it loses his smell. Suddenly, his undershirt is simply a small piece of dirty laundry. I throw it back.

I cry and tell David I'm not ready yet. David takes the undershirt back out of the basket, then Silvan's little terrycloth pajamas; he sniffs until he finds a scented corner.

"Don't sniff too much or you'll lose the scent," he warns. "And keep it out of the rest of our laundry."

I AM LYING in bed bereft, unable to move. At a loss, David goes into the other room and gets the photo album I've put together. I put it together fast, fearing that the farther I get from his death, the more difficult it will become to sift through these photos, that they will no longer seem to breathe, that they will flatten. David thinks it's strange, the way I keep looking at Silvan's photos; but he thought it was strange how much I stared at Silvan in the flesh too. He brings in the photo album and tosses it on the bed.

With nothing else to do, I pick it up.

Within minutes, I'm smiling again. I feel it on my face, a smile of wonderment. I examine Silvan's face in the photos with the same serious attention that I examined him in the flesh.

I look at each photo and try to feel as I did when the photo was taken. It's hard to believe he was always a hundred times more magnificent to me in the flesh than in his photos.

How did I manage, while he was alive, not to burst with joy?

Full Circles

FOR THIRTY-EIGHT DAYS THE PHONE RANG OFF THE hook, the world revolved around us, and nothing else happened but Silvan; but from the first morning after him, it is silent here. When someone does call, there's little to say.

Before, I had him to talk about. Now I have nothing.

For thirty-eight days, every day was April 27th, now every day is June 4th. Summer fog comes in, thick and cold, the night he dies and persists for days.

Claudia does drop by with flowers. I'd forgotten that. But there it is, in the diary that I have continued to keep. Three calla lilies, five irises still closed like exquisite brushes dipped in purple paint, an explosive pink day lily. A beautiful bouquet. Claudia produces this bouquet for us and then sits at our dining room table complaining. David asks how Brian is and she says, "He's fine. I guess. I wouldn't know. He got up this morning. He ate breakfast. No, he meditated. At any rate, he did his usual morning thing and left for work. I wouldn't know. I'm too tired. We're too busy," She says it in a flat, sarcastic voice and it's hard to tell if the dark humor is her way of relieving ordinary stress or if, in fact, there's something terribly wrong.

Now she pulls out a pack of peppermint gum.

I know what's coming. Each time she mentions her pregnancy and the nausea that has followed her right to the end, David is surprised as if he's forgotten what pregnancy looks like. But I never forget. She mentions it now, the burden of a third pregnancy. Her belly stretched beyond capacity. Next, David apologizes for the snotty tissues everywhere – those crumpled signs of grief. "Oh, please," she says, "with two kids at home, our house is snot city."

HOSPICE OFFERS FREE weekly counseling for a year after the death of a patient. For a year, we'll be able to talk about these kinds of interactions if we need to. How we and others could do this grieving thing better if we only had some rules in common. If we lived in Senegal, the whole village would be in mourning; this is what friends from Senegal tell us when it comes out that they, too, lost a child. "Here it is strange," they say. "Nobody knows." Hospice also sends us a "spiritual advisor" that first week. She comes and sits in our big armchair with a stack of books and asks questions about what kind of memorial we would like. She has ideas from all traditions, she says; she has poetry, prayers.

"Well, we have this idea…" we say and describe the sort of thing we did at our wedding, loosely based on the Quaker tradition of witnessing. We'd like our guests to stand in a circle taking turns saying whatever it is that they'd like to say about Silvan. We'd like everyone to sing Silvan's little song set to the tune of "You Are My Sunshine." We'll recite Kaddish. We'd like a Catholic prayer. In a year, we'd like to have a second ceremony, a sort of unveiling, perhaps of a child's bench that we can keep in the backyard; we will make programs for both events. As we talk, our advisor grows silent. At last, she says, "I think you'll do fine."

MY MOTHER GOES to the photocopy store with Silvan's photo to make traditional Catholic memorial cards to give out at the memorial and to send to those far away. At the store, his photo creates, in her words, "quite a stir." Employees gather around to see the beautiful baby. This is him at the peak of his beauty, hazel eyes open, fat pink lips, face bathed in golden sunlight. They all want to know if this is her beautiful grandson.

"Yes," is all she can manage.

"Why didn't you tell them the truth?" I say.

"Well…" she says and trails off with her eyebrows raised in perplexity, as if I'd asked her why she hadn't barked at them, or chirped, or mooed.

AT THE MORTICIAN'S, there's a box of tissues in the middle of the table, but no water fountain. At the mortician's, you can cry but not replenish your tears. I have been dreading it but, of course, the mortician is smooth and good, even gets me to laugh at the spelling of his Polish last name that is so much more complicated than mine.

This is a family-owned mortuary, one of the last. Because of this, they're able to tailor their prices. And because of a newborn loss within their own family, they "service" newborns at cost. He tries to sell us nothing, no coffin, no memorial urn, no spot in a crematorium. He simply tells us how much he will charge for cremation, and when we will be able to pick up "the balance of the remains."

"The balance?" David asks.

"Yes," the mortician says, "the balance of the remains."

"But what happens to the rest?"

"The rest of what?"

"Of the remains."

"You get all the balance of the remains, but I have to warn you that with a newborn it will seem shockingly little."

"But why do you keep calling them the balance of the remains?" David persists.

"Because that's what they're called."

"*All* the remains are called the *balance* of the remains?"

"Yes," the man says, refusing to explain that some of the remains may stay in the crematorium, mingled with the remains of others. Instead, he says, "No one should be sitting here in your situation. This is so rare." This doesn't seem to help.

And yet, he is probably right not to explain, not now when

Silvan still feels freshly yanked from my arms and too specific to be joined to anybody else's grief.

DAVID'S MOTHER ARRIVES in time for the memorial service. She's anxious again, unsure how to behave now that she's missed the grueling end. To get his mother to "get" it, David takes her into the office (not yet transformed into a nursery; at least we're spared that) to look at Silvan's last photos on the computer. Before David's even reached the shots where Silvan has lost weight, she's crying. I hear the sound from the living room.

"What's that noise?" Margie asks.

Margie's looking at the photo album. Like me, she loves the last photos because she remembers him like that. She likes the photo of his single pimple. Like me, she finds it cute, and proof of almost normal life.

"That noise?" I say. I go out onto the front porch.

"I think somebody's sawing," I say, coming back in.

And then I realize it's coming from the office.

Construction work. It's almost like grief. Tearing down to build again.

Hearing Linda's tears, I love her once more.

FOR THE MEMORIAL service, we've decided only to invite people who have actually met our son. Already you can predict the future course of friendships from who is there. It is a motley crowd. Our whole immediate family, of course, and our closest friends; but there are a few surprising additions, a few odd absences. Margie and Gavin are there. And Kerry, Silvan's nurse. And a pregnant friend of a friend whom we barely know but who spent hours holding Silvan at the hospital. Eve is too far away to come back so soon; for this I forgive her. But I'm not so ready to forgive Claudia and Brian. Claudia and Brian seem to think that they can neither bring their children to a memorial nor leave them at home, and I wonder if our friendship will survive it. Michael, in his second year of residency, almost makes the same mistake of being absent. He calls an hour beforehand to tell us that he can't get time off from his shift without compromising his status. He's asked his supervisor, a woman he says hates him, for a few hours off and she has been unsympathetic.

"Michael," David says, "you are in training to be a doctor who delivers babies, your best friend's baby has died due to complications of a delivery, you need to be here. This is my *son's* funeral."

An hour later, Michael arrives, swift and bashful, joining the rest of us in the backyard. Who else is there? It is a blur. We stand in a big circle on the cracked concrete beneath a rickety pergola built by the previous owners. There is not enough room in the shade so David and I stand in full sun. More than the details, I am aware of the space we hold between us, these people come to encircle us, the warmth of everyone standing in a circle on that cracked, red concrete.

We begin with the witnessing. It is sweet. People say what they can, though there's little to say about a newborn, but that is part of what I've wanted to acknowledge. I try to imitate his little cry, the one I imagined meant he wanted me. Other people mention his softness, or their sense of peace as they held him. A close friend of my mother berates the universe for giving our family so much pain, and this is nice, having her express on my behalf an anger I'm not aware of feeling. I tell everyone I am forever grateful that I got what mattered most to me. "Silvan died in my arms," I say.

We must have sung; we must have recited prayers – I have a program to prove it.

And yet my memory of it feels vague. It is a memory of memory becoming vague. I fail to record it in my diary. David tells me later that other people liked it, that his father told him we did a nice job. And I do remember feeling buoyed, completed. To dedicate this time entirely to this little being is incredible. But it is also incredibly little compared to the life he could have lived. To think that all we have left are these tiny stories is painful.

To think that never again will so many people remember him so well…

AFTERWARDS, WE "SIT shiva." Though we have broken all sorts of Jewish rules by performing an autopsy and cremating Silvan, how glad we are for the ritual of shiva. How else would we carry on? We need time for organized grief. Our shiva is modified from the seven days immediately following burial to a two-day shiva happening on the weekend so more people can come. We don't know much about sitting shiva, nor do our friends, but one thing I learn is that the bereaved are not required to stand at the arrival of each guest. It is a good rule. I'm too tired to stand. I don't have it in me to give that much attention to others. Instead, I announce to each person who arrives, "The rules of shiva say I don't have to stand."

Another thing I learn is that you only sit shiva for people older than thirty days. This is interesting considering that a neonatal death is defined as occurring earlier than twenty-eight days. So Silvan is considered more than a newborn both medically and spiritually. I wonder if my grief, and the grief of our family and friends, would have been any different had he died at twenty-eight days instead of thirty-eight. My grief for Silvan feels so particular – no one else in the world can miss him as much as I do – but ritual helps remind me that I'm not the only mother who has grieved.

All sorts of unexpected people come. A friend from high school. Two former students. I'm most touched by two men from work. They're both awkward, both thin with big old-fashioned glasses and unruly hair that gets cut at most once a year; they are older than me, poorer, single, childless. But they come all this way to my house to stand in my backyard and hold photos of my dead baby and say appropriate things like, "I am so sorry for your loss."

Neighbors come and stand awkwardly at the edge of the shade. We have only lived in this neighborhood five months, but still they stand there and look at Silvan's photo album, thumbing quickly through the final pages because they are too awful. How odd that I subject them to this. What do I want? Isn't it enough that they are here?

One neighbor is wearing a beautiful dress, kaleidoscopic, and I take pleasure in telling her how much I admire it.

My obstetrician is there.

My chiropractor's receptionist with a little potted plant.

More neighbors arrive with a bottle of wine and sit easily with my mother and pass the time of day with her.

As shiva goes on, more people we know less well arrive, and more food comes with them. Piles of cakes and cookies. Dozens of doughnuts. Everything sweet. By Sunday night, as people leave, we're begging them to take sweet things away with them.

Monday morning comes, and the house feels strangely empty. We uncover each mirror. We take a first symbolic walk outside. I feel raw and exposed but glad again for rituals to mark the resumption of life. We circle back to the front porch where we have lit a memorial candle. It's on the little table where Silvan's body once lay. The candle is supposed to burn for seven days, but since we have modified our shiva, I think we should blow it out. David says he'll do whatever I want, but when I try to blow out the candle, my breath is undirected, broken by tears. We leave it burning. We go back into the house.

We drag through the remaining days of that week and on the seventh day, sometime in the night, I wake again searching the bed for Silvan. At least what I'm saying is, "Where's Silvan? Where's Silvan?" but in my semi-sleep I'm searching for Silvan's babies, a tray of two of them.

In the morning, we find the candle has gone out.

Fledglings

WHEN OTHERS DIED, I HAD A SENSE OF SOULS THAT lingered longer. I felt my father watching with approval from above. I felt Mark arriving in the body of an owl to forgive me for not having noticed the bathroom ceiling. But Silvan was so unformed that within days there seems nothing left. I continue waking in the night, patting down the bed, touching only absence. What baby am I looking for? "Olive?" I say, but Olive is Eve's baby. "Oscar?" but Oscar is Margie's. David wakes and reminds me, "Silvan is gone."

Yes, he's gone. With relief, I lie back down. Silvan no longer needs me.

With relief, I accept that I'm the one left to suffer, not him.

Around this time, a friend gives me a book of "comforting faiths" – as if faith were a sweater in a catalogue, something to be ordered and tried on for size – and I read how some women like to believe that their babies' souls have returned to be reborn, sometimes into the same wombs. I'm not comforted at all. I am enraged. If the faith of my youth has dissipated, it is not to be replaced by some other faith. Silvan has had his life. Silvan is gone. And now that Silvan is gone, it is as Dr. Z used to say, we don't regret a minute that we had with him.

But in his absence, I'm also unformed, a mother who is childless.

Unformed, the two of us drift around the house, David and I, like newlyweds, strangely insulated from the world. David's mother returns home, our families and friends return to the lives they were living before. Because we were grieving for all of Silvan's life, because we were fed and cared for during all that time, people seem to feel they've done enough. I understand. I am ready to be alone again. When my mother calls to ask if I am okay, I say, "I'm fine." When she doesn't seem to believe me, I go on, "Losing a grown son to suicide is probably worse than losing a newborn." I don't know if you can compare grief this way, but I sense more life ahead than my mother once did, after Mark died and I found her crying at the bottom of the basement stairs.

Slowly, David and I begin to tidy, to nest, to clear away the patient plastic bags that have lain in a corner of the dining room since the day after Silvan's birth. At least we don't have a full nursery to dismantle. At least we don't find baby accessories objectively attractive. With each item that I remove, glider, bassinet, changing table, the house looks better. It is a reverse sort of nesting. The only toy I keep visible is the white angel bear with the iridescent wings and halo that my obstetrician gave us.

The bassinet in the corner of our bedroom is replaced with a good luck money tree brought over by a neighbor who scuttles away after delivering it. He also lost a newborn, he tells us, a boy he had decided should be spared a grueling, risky heart surgery. This affords him entry into our house. From the house on the other side, a neighbor emerges to tell us that her twin nephews died as newborns too. In the newspaper, David reads that our zip code has the highest infant mortality rate in the state. This may have nothing to do with the particular damage Silvan sustained, but it connects us somehow, all these islands of grief, all these grieving parents who might understand us.

On our tidier island, we cook simple meals. We talk to friends on the phone. We continue talking to the social worker about what we expect from our friends and what we feel we are failing to get. Claudia comes over now that the memorial and shiva are over and says we need a new sofa. She thinks our sofa –

the sofa of David's childhood – is more ugly and uncomfortable than grieving parents should have to bear. Her anger about people not getting what they "deserve" repels me. No one deserves anything, I think. The sofa *is* ugly and uncomfortable. Someday I want to replace it, but certainly not now when I'm working on simply being grateful for what we have left. For one thing, the stack of photos – the extras from the memorial. They sit on the dresser by my open bedroom window. It is an impractical spot, but I must like how the summer wind keeps Silvan present as I go about tidying. He flits around, making a mess in my mind.

"Here I am," his picture says from beside my slippers on the closet floor.

"Here I am," he says floating down before the mirror.

THAT FIRST WEEK after he's gone, I barely leave the bedroom. I lie there with his photo album, I close my eyes and dream about him.

Next, I leave the house but only for the yard.

Next, I walk around the neighborhood.

Little by little, I fly farther and farther from the nest.

I try dinner at a restaurant with David. That doesn't go well. Looking at a happy young couple at the next table, I begin to cry. David takes my hand. I cry harder. We must look like we're breaking up and my sobs come harder, thinking no one can see through my grief to the child who has brought us so close together.

Next, I go for a haircut. My haircutter has heard the news from Eve whose job it was to call everyone. She says she is surprised how good I look, considering. "It's because," I say, "he gave me so much joy." I have not formulated that thought out loud before and it strikes me as sad; it's as incommunicable as grief, my joy. I catch sight of my reflection in the mirror and it's not joy I see but something more complicated peering out from under my wet hair. I see both pride and ugly shame, and shy hope.

A few days later, I go on a hike with my sister. While we

are gone, someone smashes a window and steals everything in my trunk, including my purse. The policeman who takes the report wants me to list everything I've lost. Nothing I've lost seems to impress him. It was a trunk full of junk, old blankets we kept there in case we needed to sleep at the hospital with Silvan, a breast pumping kit, a coat, a pair of heels. Not even the loss of my purse impresses him, an old ripped cloth bag with an old cellphone in it. In the purse I also had a notebook in which I took some of my notes about Silvan, but this impresses him least of all. Desperate, I say, "And all my photos of my dead son."

He does not react at all.

When he's gone, I tell my sister I made up that last part about the photos.

She is shocked. "Why would you make that up?"

I shrug. "I wanted him to feel my pain."

And it's true, I can scarcely keep the pain to myself.

Thinking we're ready, we respond at last to the doula's messages. We invite her to come over. We sit on the sofa and try to tell her the whole story starting from the night she left the hospital. She says, "I'm not a doctor, but…" and tries to blame the doctor for what happened next. When I don't take the bait, she asks if there's anything I regret. Thinking she wants my advice on how to be a better doula, I say I wish I hadn't spent so much time in the shower because I felt Silvan's last kick there.

"Most women love showers," she says, her face blank. So I give her a check and ask for the photo of Silvan she took at birth. "I had it, but I couldn't bear to look at it," she says, "so I put it in a drawer and now I can't find it."

I wait. I want her to say she'll look for it. I want her to treasure Silvan's memory as we do. I resist seeing that, although I have something for her, she has nothing at all for me.

HAVING GRIEVED BEFORE – having practiced on flies and old men, having lost a brother, a father, a friend – does not make me immune. It only makes me more patient, perhaps, with the feeling – the dry mouth, the foggy head, the sense of isolation. I watch myself, bemused, as I tell the man at the shoe store that my son has just died. Next, I try and fail to stop myself from telling the couple with the stroller. I watch their eyebrows shoot up, I hear their flat words of condolence; I see that this is my need, not theirs, but I can't stop. Telling people seems to help.

In late June, the gauze unwinds a little. With relief, I feel the pain of others again; I feel for my friend in New Mexico who tells me at last that her husband has left her; I commiserate with another who's just learned that the treatment of her arthritis may have rendered her infertile.

Tender and exposed, I decide to give up my writing. I decide to give up my teaching, too, and my part-time night job. I will do something more useful. Perhaps I will become a grief counselor and in that way make use of my pain. But the social worker who still visits us from hospice counsels against it. "It's better not to make major life changes while in the midst of grief," she says.

Meanwhile, I continue writing in my diary. How patient David is with my need. I write frantically in the diary as if Silvan's scent is in the ink, as if I am afraid to let that scent go dry. I fill notebook after notebook, and then, thinking the thicket of my handwriting may repel my return to these pages in the future, I force myself to type them out. Hundreds of typed pages, and still I don't go back to my "real" work.

A colleague calls, wondering if I will return. "I want you to know," she says, "I agree with your choice. It's natural. Think of birds, they abandon fledglings that don't fly. They do it for the sake of the species."

I want to agree, but it's not that simple.

There is no one way for a parent to act. Nor is there one way to grieve.

If I can shape Silvan's life and death into a story, I can survive it. If I can hear that I was brave, that I was loving, then the story makes sense. I want confirmation that we have made the right choice. I want the story to fit into the story of my life.

God may never have appeared to me in a shaft of light to tell me what to do, but still there is a voice inside me, a voice that believes Silvan's time has come and gone while the rest of us have to go on living.

WE GO ON living with a simple walk around the neighborhood each night after dinner in the safety of dusk. It is July, David has been off work for two months, and now he's back and scrambling to catch up. Margie tells us that at her job she's put Silvan's face up as a screensaver. How moved I am to think that when Margie turns from her desk to pump milk for her own baby, Silvan's face floats up angelic. David's boss, on the other hand, has sent an email to the company asking people not to bother David with personal questions. Though David approved his boss's request, it has been much harder than he imagined. He comes home squashed by the silence.

If only he could talk about Silvan at work, he says, it would feel more natural to be there. If only people would listen. We walk around the neighborhood brimming with our story. At the same time, David is moving on. He wants to buy a car. Though I refuse to shop for a sofa, I concede that our car is on its last legs. I don't oppose his research. It gives him something to focus on.

One night as we stroll, David spots a car of the type he wants. It's a family car, a station wagon, a safe and optimistic choice. He urges me to come and look up close. Peering in with my hands cupped to the passenger window, I see a car seat. I jump back as if singed. The car seat is blue. It is stamped with puppies' feet. It is the exact model we bought for Silvan still boxed in our garage.

"It's not fair," I say.

"What do you mean it's not fair?" David says, sounding like my father. "We have that exact same car seat."

We break into morbid laughter.

David takes my hand and kisses it and as we step away from the car, we notice a couple of birds. They hop and trill at us in shrill staccato. We suspect a baby bird must be nearby but we aren't prepared to find one. There it is, right in front of us on the sidewalk, squashed flat. We stop.

"That's the sound of bird grief," David finally says.

I nod. We don't know if it's true, but I wish I had the language to comfort them.

I take David's hand again. We walk along, linked.

Mutation

MY MOTHER POSTPONES RETIREMENT, MY SISTER RETURNS to Brazil, my brother reschedules his wedding from this summer to the following, and I am relieved as if this repetition all around me means that I can remain here circling like a bird in the sky; but at last, David convinces me. Three months ago, we were in the Bad News Room together and I was asking him not to let this ruin our marriage, and he was asking me to have another child again someday; so now we're in that future time together trying to move beyond what feels like the tragic climax of my life. Perhaps there have been other times since Silvan was born, but this is the first sex I remember after him.

It is mid-July. Though some people counsel against getting pregnant again until one has grieved "fully," I know I will grieve Silvan whether I'm pregnant or not. And anyway, if I want to get pregnant again, my doctor recommends not waiting any longer because of my age and history. So I lie back and David cups the back of my head in his palm. This is how I used to hold Silvan. I close my eyes and, just as I used to confuse my own nose with Silvan's while he was alive, now my whole body is Silvan's body, and David is me, and we are all one, making love, as we were in the moment of Silvan's conception, and I can't do it.

"Stop," I say.

David stops, but he is disappointed.

"This feels," I say, "like a betrayal of Silvan."

David shakes his head. "When will you be ready?" he asks.

I don't know.

WHILE WAITING TO know if I can do this, I make the mistake of going to see Claudia and Brian. Their third child has been born and they're having a belated baby shower. I must want to prove to myself that, though they failed to be strong enough for a memorial, I'm strong enough for the optimism of a shower. The women sit around comparing labors. I want to chime in. I want to say, "Mine was sixteen hours," or "I only needed two stitches" but the end of my story seems to overshadow the joy of its beginning. Everyone avoids my eyes. Then a well-meaning friend leans over and says, "You'll see. The joy when you have your next child will amaze you," and I wonder what part of my joy in Silvan she has missed.

I accept the little bundled baby being passed around the room. He has the same weight and warmth as Silvan, only this baby is as floppy as a ragdoll. In that moment, I realize how strangely stiff Silvan had been, his brain already failing to show him how to move. I have to hand the baby swiftly on, which is fine because Claudia beckons me into the kitchen. She wants to tell me a story about her neighbor down the street, as if I'm best equipped to deal with this story. She leans in close to tell me how he was lying there in his lawn chair as he usually did but he'd already "passed."

She says this so softly I'm not sure I've heard right. "You mean he was dead?"

"Shh," Claudia says. She indicates her older children jumping off the sofa in the next room. "They don't know that word yet."

I say, "But what about death itself? Surely they know about that?" but she only shrugs vaguely. It's the vagueness that gets me. Though it feels almost as wrong as death to do so, in that moment I let our friendship go. If I'm lucky, I think, someday I'll have children who will know about death. They will puzzle over birds who crash into our windows and lie broken-necked on the stairs. They will know that chicken comes from chickens and beef from cows. They will study the glassy eyes of fish at the market. Sometimes they will be the ones to kill things themselves and ask if they are really dead. They will keep a pet snail in a cage for too long and when they find it foamy and tucked tight in its shell, they will cry the way I cried over pets as a child and then be relieved when they take it outside to see it revive and creep away into a shelter of dead leaves. They will know that many people I have loved are dead and that the real dead stay dead.

THE DOCTORS SAY it's statistically improbable, but once you've been on the wrong end of statistics, statistics don't matter so much. At least not to me. To David, statistics are comforting, which is why he's ready; but even still he has to admit that statistics don't address the heart of the question that remains. Could we let another child die? Even if it's highly unlikely it would happen again, we have to ask ourselves what we would do. Even if we thought it was the right choice before, we're not sure we'd have the strength to endure it again. I've been reading a book about neonatal ethics and stumbled across a palliative care nurse who'd like to establish the equivalent of a living will for babies so that parents who are pregnant start preparing themselves for the possibility of something going wrong. And yet I can see how hard it would be to introduce the topic of death to women like Claudia who seem to have the luxury of separating thoughts of birth from death when it's hard even for us to think about a baby dying.

At the same time as I hesitate, grimly asking myself these questions about birth and death, we've continued doing tests to figure out what happened to Silvan. The autopsy has found nothing wrong with his body. His asphyxiation during labor remains unexplained. It could happen again just as it could happen to anyone. Still, we continue exploring possible reasons that it occurred and that's how my obstetrician comes up with the unexpected results of a genetic mutation that I carry on both sides of my genes. As a hematologist friend of a friend says (as transmitted to us in a suspect game of telephone), "It's amazing she carried a baby to term at all and survived."

My doctor sends us to a hematologist for a consultation. He sits on the other side of a shiny desk with his plaque and family photos all around him. He gets out a study, something we've found ourselves online, that talks about my genetic mutation. He reiterates what we know: I have a higher chance not only of stillbirth or dying myself postpartum of a clot, but it's also highly unlikely that a fertilized egg will implant itself in my womb. He's distant and vague about our chances of having a child and I want him to care.

"Would you like to see the baby we lost?" I ask, holding out a picture of Silvan.

"No," he says loudly, flinging up his arms. But it's too late, there he is, Silvan, angelic in the sunlight, and the doctor sees him, sidelong; then he turns a portrait on his desk so we can see his daughter. He smiles.

So I ask him. "What do you think our chances are?"

The smiles goes away. He looks grim. "I can't promise anything."

I am stunned. I'm not asking for a *promise*. I'm not asking for empty hope. Even I know, since I've already carried a healthy baby to term, that I have a chance. I want that chance, that basis for hope, broken down statistically. I get a second referral. This doctor is known nationally for his work in both hematology and obstetrics. I say to him, "I've never had a blood clot, nor have either of my parents. My mother carried three children to term. I carried Silvan to term. Where's the proof that this condition is a problem for me?" I'm thinking of the family tree hanging outside my grandfather's nursing home room in Bromley, Kent, a tree that goes back hundreds of years and wondering how many of those women lost babies. I'm also thinking of the bird couple David and I saw, trilling and hopping before the body of their dead fledgling as though grieving. I'm thinking of my friend who said she admired birds who abandon fledglings for the sake of their species. I feel strangely liberated from myself; I feel like an animal determined to reproduce.

And to my surprise, the doctor smiles. He says, "So far, we have only been able to study women who are symptomatic." In fact, what happened to Silvan probably has nothing to do with my "condition," he says. What happened to Silvan remains a mystery, just something that happens in labor sometimes. He asks only that I consider, if I don't want to be on blood thinners all through my next pregnancy, to give myself subcutaneous shots for six weeks after the baby is born since this is a peak time for clotting. In this way, he gives his blessing to go ahead and try. "Because you're right, of course. We have no idea how many women like you there are out there."

On the way home, David tells me he is definitely ready to try again. He believes we will be able to have more children. But after my heady moment in the doctor's office, the reality of pregnancy overwhelms me. I say, "I'm not sure I can handle being pregnant." Suddenly, the weight and anxiety of nurturing a baby inside of me, of being the only one who can keep it alive, of facing the possibility of another death seems too much again. "But you won't even know at first that you're pregnant," David says; and I say, "But I will." And then, in the middle of the bridge, in the middle of five lanes of traffic, the strength returns. Babies die, I think. Mothers die. These things *still happen* and women *like me* still go ahead and try.

Crows

WE TRY IN AUGUST; AND WITHIN DAYS I FEEL MY NIPPLES tingle in the shower. I know I should be grateful, but within the first flush of pregnancy, there is bitterness. Silvan has only been gone since June. Back in April, I was still pregnant with him. With only four months between pregnancies, I feel like a mother whale who must gestate for eighteen months just to produce one child. I feel disloyal to both babies. My morning sickness extends for months beyond what's considered normal. My back is already giving out as if I've never stopped carrying a baby. In the classroom teaching writing once more, I feel like a fraud; whenever I try to write a word beyond my diary, my mind goes blank. I find half my students know what happened, half don't. Those who don't must think I'm strangely reticent about what's obviously happening inside my body. I feel as if a nail is being driven into the top of my head.

That fall, I endure various tests to determine if the baby is developing fine. That fall, crows also move into the neighborhood, fat ominous crows. If one flies over my head alone, I am all right. One seems a symbol of Silvan. But if two fly overhead, I worry that this means two babies will die, Silvan and another. If three, I think perhaps David and I will have one more, to make us a family of three. Or perhaps three babies will die. I take almost as much stock in superstition as in tests.

At the drugstore, a week before the amniocentesis, a clerk asks the sex of the baby, and when I say I don't yet know, she tells me to visualize whatever sex I want. "It worked for my sister," she says, "three times." Back home, I rant against the clerk and her arrogant assumption of power over the randomness of nature, and David teases me. "You should have told her you used to picture giving birth without actually having to raise the baby and how that worked, too." How I love the darkness of his humor.

From the amnio, we learn the baby is a boy. That is a relief, that I'm carrying something familiar. At the gym, a woman rushes up and puts her hands on my belly. "Don't I sometimes wish my children were still inside. They're so much less work there." I glare at her, scarcely able to contain myself from telling her how much work it is to carry a baby you fear may not survive.

A neighbor overflows with empathy. "I've been thinking," she says, "of you back at the gym, going to your dance class. That must be hard, going back to a place where everyone watches each others' bodies, where everyone must think you already have a baby at home."

How grateful I am to anyone who knows, to anyone who understands.

Right after Silvan died, I sent a friend ahead to show a picture of me and Silvan to my dance teacher, so she would know. I hadn't wanted her to rush over to congratulate me before class. Instead, she'd hugged me long and hard after class, our bodies touching in the space where I had danced Silvan as a fetus around the room, even in my final week, the two of us born aloft on my certain hope.

As I get bigger this time, I still dance. I dance my grief, my fear through my body and I avoid the eager eyes of strangers. No public revelry over my fecund dancing for me this time, thank you. "Your first?" strangers inevitably ask. I stumble over the answer. "Not exactly," or "Kind of," I say, allowing them to fill in the mystery however they like. I am still grieving; I am not yet rejoicing. How hard it is to prepare for both everything and nothing to change. I refuse to say when I expect my baby to be born without adding humbly, "I hope."

TWICE A WEEK starting in the third trimester, I drive to the hospital to lie on a bed with a monitor strapped to me, listening to the heartbeat, because my doctor wants to make sure this new baby doesn't die inside. Though I feel confident, I know he could die. The nurses are also confident, and they also know he could die. On the other side of the country, Eve is also pregnant with her second; she wants her midwife to tell the truth about labor this time, that sometimes even healthy babies die in labor and the midwife admits, "It's true. It can happen to anyone; it has even happened to babies I have delivered." I lie on the bed strapped to the monitor, counting his kicks, waiting for the nurses to say everything is fine.

This time my obstetrician makes a commitment to me. No matter what, she will be the one to deliver this baby. To ensure this, her family bends their vacation schedules to the softening of my cervix, to the descent of my baby. She waits until she thinks my body is ready, and then she breaks my water because she wants the labor to begin in the hospital where she can monitor it. She is right about my body being ready. Within a minute, the pains start, as they did with Silvan, and my labor progresses naturally once more. I've made a note for my chart that I plan to labor without drugs, but that I'm also ready for any intervention to save this baby.

The nurses who surround me are handpicked by my doctor and they are soothing and efficient. This time, I wear a wireless fetal monitor that is much in demand by other patients because it's portable. With the portable monitor, I can wander the halls while the nurses continue hearing the baby's heartbeat. My doctor wants me monitored for every second of the labor, but she doesn't want me to feel burdened by my monitor. She doesn't want me to keep asking to take it off the way I did with Silvan.

My new doula is everything she should be, attentive, patient and calm. A help to the nurses but not a replacement for them. She has been a doula for thirty years and has seen babies die, has seen mothers go ahead and give birth again. This is why we have picked her. Because she can deal. She can even adjust the belt of the monitor in a way that hardly bothers me. We have made her promise not to suggest a shower. There is still no explanation for what happened to Silvan, but it's enough that I am here in the same hospital without having to step into the same shower. So she never suggests a shower, she rubs my legs for hours, she marvels that I can labor without drugs while preserving my sense of humor. We laugh and everything seems manageable and fine until my doctor walks in and notices the heartbeat.

It is half the speed it should be.

How long has this been happening? Who has failed to notice?

They all go into action, the nurses adjusting my body, preparing equipment, my doctor reaching inside me to screw a different monitor to the baby's head … and then there is a new sound, higher, faster.

"Is that him?" I ask.

No one hears me. They are busying themselves with more instruments.

"Is he damaged?" I ask again. "Is that him?"

Finally, my doctor hears. She says, "Yes, that's him. He sounds fine. He's just too far down the birth canal for the other monitor to work. We were hearing your heart instead, but you need to push now."

"Okay," I say as if this is simple; and I push.

"Now wait," she says. She unwinds the cord that happens to be around his neck. "Now push," she says and I push and David catches the baby, cuts the cord, and lays him on my chest. I'm watching myself from a distance, as if this baby lying on my chest is miles away. "Terminal meconium," I hear the doctor reporting to the nurse. Seeing my face, my doctor says, "By 'terminal' I mean 'at the end,' I mean the kind that's okay because it only happened at the very end of his birth. I mean, he's fine."

I lie there, baby on my chest, waiting to see if I can love him.

THE BABY IS asleep in his bassinet in the living room. We have not named him yet. We can't name him yet. We don't know who he is or how long he will be here. I sit on the toilet and weep: I want Silvan back. That's the first week after birth.

THEN AGAIN, THERE is his first bath. We fill the tub in the sink, he squirms and turns pink, and when we get him out and dry him, he moves his eyes from side to side, alert and eager and exquisite, and then he sneezes. David catches the sneeze on video, and we watch the video over and over. "He's so cute," I say every time.

WE TAKE A week to do it, but at last we name him Miles in public acknowledgement of Miles Davis and in private memory of my brother Mark.

WHEN MILES IS one month old, my mother retires, my sister returns from Brazil for good, and my brother Kim gets married. I wear my orange silk wedding shawl and hide Miles under it to nurse during the special ceremony Kim's wife has secretly prepared as part of the reception. Having changed from her white wedding dress, Gretel dresses as a Korean bride and comes to serve us tea in a ceremony that signifies the joining of our families. How random, how agonizingly beautiful is the making of families, Kim's birth mother giving him up, Silvan dying, Kim becoming ours, Miles arriving, Gretel joining us to her family. Even David's family is represented at the wedding. His mother has just returned to New Jersey after a visit, but his father and stepmother are there, his sister and her boyfriend. There are pictures of us all on the dance floor, expanding.

THREE MONTHS LATER, once I've stopped giving myself subcutaneous shots against blood clotting and it seems both Miles and I are really here to stay, Eve flies out with her husband and two daughters to go camping with us. We have a briefcase-sized bed

for Miles that we lay between our sleeping bags, but we are un-
prepared for a night in the Sierra. Each time I touch Miles, his
nose and hands seem cooler. I already have him in three layers of
clothes and under two blankets and then I add my down vest as
a blanket. This is exactly what you are told not to do, I think, bury
him in blankets. Though I am trying to become an ordinary
parent who can go camping easily with her child, I decide I must
just stay up to watch him breathe in the moonlight. To make
sure he doesn't stop. But then I drift off, and when I next wake, I
reach out to touch him. His hand is frozen stiff.

"Miles," I shout into the night.

He stirs.

Three times that night, I wake and shake him.

"Leave him alone," David finally counsels.

At dawn, I awaken again, disbelieving that Miles can still be
asleep, that he will ever be awake again. I am heaved up onto
my elbow, watching his face, when the sun rises over the hills. It
pierces the canopy of live oak leaves overhead and filters softly
down onto his face. His eyes spring open. He stares up at the
leaves. I see their lacey patterns on his eyes. He beams. I sit up
to nurse him and listen to the brook murmuring past. I feel
both Miles' warm weight in my arms and the absence of Silvan,
amazed I can feel both extremes at once.

"THERE'S NOTHING LIKE the joy of parents," our hospice
social worker says back in Berkeley, "at the birth of a subsequent
child." Having exceeded her limit of one year, she comes a final
time just to bring a gift for Miles.

How moved I am to know that Miles is as special as Silvan.

In fact, as if the world knows of our grief and how special
Miles is because of it, stranger after stranger comes up to us. Even
in front of other women's babies, they say crazy, exuberant
things: "I'm not a baby person usually, but your child is perfect…"
or "Your baby seems unusually wise…" or "always cheerful" or
"Here's the card for my talent agent." It's as if Miles is a reflection,

a distillation of our joy. Or perhaps he's got charisma in his own right. It certainly seems that way.

One day, I'm out eating with a friend, both of us with toddlers. Miles is keeping me busy, grabbing cutlery, napkins, wanting to stand on my chair, sit on the floor, pick at old food. In between, I feed myself, listen to my friend. There's no room for anything else.

But suddenly, a grumpy-looking old man at the next table leans over.

"What did you ever do," he asks me, and I'm sure from his face that he's going to criticize our messy presence here, but he concludes, "to get such a wonderful child?"

What I want to answer stops my tongue. "He was sent to me, as recompense," I want to say as if I believe life works this way; instead, I say, "It wasn't easy," sounding like any mother, stunned by the weight and ecstasy of love.

STUNNED BY THE weight and ecstasy of love, I want more, more, more.

But if we try again, David warns me, this time he will not be so attentive, he will not give so many foot rubs; and he is true to his word. But at least the third pregnancy is easier. When people ask, "Is this your first?" it's easier to tell the truth by saying, "I have an older one at home." Usually the person asking says, "Your second!" anyway, but I don't correct them even though inside I'm screaming, "My third!"

It will be another boy, we learn. I've always wanted a girl, but now I'm relieved that I'm having only boys. If I keep having boys like Silvan, I seem to think I will miss him less. I'm unaware of this thinking until the birth – which is easy, I feel like a pioneer woman popping babies out – when the baby emerges not at all dark like Silvan or Miles or David. Ivan has pale skin and pink cheeks and blond curly hair like my own baby hair and Katya's and my father's before that. I stare down at him on my chest and say, "Is he cute?" Again there is that distance between me and him, the distance I did not feel from Silvan, though Silvan was already far away from me, across the room. "Look how alert he is," the attending pediatrician says with pleasure, trying to make me feel good. "Babies born without drugs are so wonderful." When I don't react, she repeats herself. "Babies born without drugs are great. You did a good job."

I lie there holding this wonderful baby and wondering how many more children I have inside, how many more children I need to give birth to before I can get Silvan back.

IVAN SUFFERS FROM being not just a second, but a third baby. He has two older siblings competing for my attention. Two *first-born* siblings. As if he senses he can't compete, he cries all the time. He wakes easily in the night. Strangers do not flock to him, except to compliment his curly locks. Blessed with a third son, I wonder if I have wished for the wrong thing after all. It almost seems like a mistake, becoming an ordinary, irritated mother, swabbing at pee running down the wall in the dining room, carting a baby and a toddler, both screaming, one in each arm, for blocks.

My mother says she warned me, but I don't remember her warning. She makes up for this by taking my boys for hours. When she returns them to me, they smell both like themselves and like her; this heady broth nestles in the crooks of their necks, and I sniff and sniff at it. Pleasure now has to be measured by the thimbleful such as this, for without crisis, life threatens to become ordinary. I am frustrated once more with David's inarticulate hesitance in talk about movies and books, and he remembers how selfish I can be with my time. With every sentence interrupted, and no meal eaten without the passing of a baby back and forth, or the dropping of a fork, or the spilling of a glass, no night unbroken, we feel almost nothing but misery. There seems not room enough for love. Passing a friend in our no-longer-new family station wagon, David rolls down his window. We have not seen this friend since the birth of their second baby. But there he is, pushing a double stroller. "How's life?" David calls out.

Our friend looks up, bleary-eyed. "Great!"

I yell across David, "Well, we're in hell!"

Our friend grins in relief. "So are we."

I have arrived. I can use language sloppily, without apology or contrition. I, who once did not know if I could have any children, can say that having two children is "hell" without qualifying that I have actually had three, or that losing one child is more hellish than raising two. I have become a parent like any other, the miracle of my young children almost buried in all the work.

Sunshine

AS TIME PASSES, AS THE LONG DAYS OF SILVAN'S DYING shrink proportionally against the growing of my children – soon they are one and three, then two and four – I catch glimpses of Silvan in other women's pregnant bellies, painful glimpses, fleeting glimpses. At baby showers, I find I still can't grow giddy with the other mothers over the certainty that soon a baby will be here. The farther my children get from their own babyhoods, the harder it is to hold new babies and smell that distantly familiar smell. In every six-week-old, I lose Silvan all over again.

Spring is the hardest. April 27th to June 4th. Every year, I spend those days in vague dread over an end we have already lived through. On one of those spring days – a lovely, balmy one – I am sitting on a park bench, chatting with the other parents when I notice Miles lying splayed on the sand, unblinking, staring straight up. Perhaps he is dead. A dead child is not something I have to imagine. My heart begins to beat wildly. Perhaps, I tell myself, trying to stay calm, he is merely playing dead to get my attention, to see how I will love him if he dies as his brother did. Suddenly, I am alone, no other parents near, though they sit beside me on the bench. "Miles," I say with quiet urgency, "Stop it."

To my great relief, he's alive. To my greater relief, he listens. He gets up and returns to activities that bother me less but probably bother the other parents more, throwing rocks, balancing large plastic toys on the tops of the monkey bars below which Ivan and the other younger children play. Like any parent,

I worry about my children dying. Like most parents, I try to live as though they won't.

AS THE WORK eases slightly, as dinner becomes somewhat civilized again, we begin to look for rituals to bind us. We start by lighting candles every Friday night. This is not about a god so much as it is about pausing to be grateful. How grateful I am, how hard to pass gratitude on. Usually we're tired on Friday nights and the children wiggle and giggle until we yell at them to stop, but surely they can find something to be grateful for. We make suggestions. David suggests they feel grateful for the meal I've cooked. I suggest they feel grateful for having food at all. This gives them pause, as it should. For they know about death. They have seen dead flies and snails, they know that their older brother is gone.

Their questions start early, startling me.

"What if Silvan were in this box?" Miles asks one Christmas – for we celebrate that ritual, too – over a present he's opening at my mother's.

"Why would he be in a box?" I ask.

"Wouldn't you like that?" he asks.

A few years later, Ivan pipes up from the backseat of the car. "What if Silvan comes back to life? Would you like that?"

"People don't come back to life," I tell him.

"Maybe," he says.

"Maybe," I concede because it's true; I don't know what's possible.

In dance class, I'm stunned one evening by a vision of Silvan and me and centuries of dead, pressed up against each other in the dark, at the edge of an underground stream. I don't know if I believe in souls that way anymore, but I am in awe of all that a mind can contain, more than we will ever know.

If I could, I would hold Silvan again.

But for now, I have only his ashes in a vase in the living room – after scattering a few on the trail where once I imagined his conception, I couldn't let the rest go. And in a drawer, his pale-blue terrycloth pajamas. And I have his bench in the backyard. It's a child-sized wooden bench, a plaque attached to the back of it with his dates and a quote from his song, the one we used to sing to him. "You'll never know dear," the bench says, "how much we love you…" Over time, the bench has become hidden. To find it now, you have to cross to a back corner of the yard, walk up three little stairs of stone, and duck beneath the drooping flowers of an angel trumpet. That was our idea, a hidden place to find if you make the effort. A place to sit and love him.

Often it is children who find it first. They lead their unsuspecting parents there. When the adults reemerge from under the plants, I wait to see if they will say something.

Some do, some don't.

And then one day, I find I can forgive those who don't. Not everyone has to know.

Sometimes even I forget, if only for an hour.

In April, Margie tells me, "I had my Silvan dream last night, I always dream about him this time of year. Is it okay I told you that?"

Yes, of course, I say.

A few days later, I run into Dr. A. He lives in our neighborhood. "Wasn't it Silvan's birthday yesterday?" he asks.

Yes, I say, yes.

Every birthday, David's sister makes a donation to children's hospice in his memory; and David's stepmother calls to thank us for being brave enough to have more children. At my brother's house, I see Silvan's picture. At my obstetrician's office, too. There he is golden amongst a swirl of babies. If there is a miracle to this story, it is that he is remembered. Not by everyone, but by enough. He is my boy, so specifically mine; but in death he can belong to anyone who wants him.

I NO LONGER have to tell everyone about Silvan – but my willingness to offer his story remains. One winter morning almost seven years from his birth, I return to the diaries I kept while he was alive. From my diaries, I retrieve the feel of his skin, the sound of his little cries. I retrieve both the joy and the agony. I find the story of his life. Memory begets memory and within days I know I'm writing a book. Within months, I have a draft. And that fall, when the book is almost ready to be seen, I find myself out in the backyard with my boys on a hot afternoon drenched in yellow sunshine. I am pruning jasmine from Silvan's bench while the boys dig a giant hole nearby. Where the hole will lead them, they don't know, but they've been digging in earnest for over a year. How content I suddenly am, but also worried about my own contentedness. If I end Silvan's story with children in the sunshine, will I have failed to tell the truth about losing him?

That's when I hear them arguing over by their hole.

Ivan wants to talk about what he will do when he is twelve, and Miles is reminding him that he might not live to be twelve. After all, "Silvan didn't."

"Yesss…" Ivan shouts with four-year-old vehemence.

"But you can't know for sure," Miles says smugly, "right Mommy?"

"That's true," I say, "but…"

"I know," Ivan interrupts, "but I just want to tell you what I'm going to do."

"Okay," Miles gives in, and they begin to talk about their future without any reassurance from me until Ivan reminds Miles that I may not live into that future. Now Miles is upset. As I hesitate behind them, trying to find a balance between hope and truth, Ivan says, "One thing you can know for sure is that she's still alive right now."

"Now that is true," I say, and they turn to beam at me.

As I beam back, I know something else for sure. Love outlasts grief. Though we can't say for certain we made the right choice for Silvan, our love for him has survived. It is alive this very minute. How lucky I feel. And how full of hope. For I feel it now, hope fluttering up. David comes out of the house to join us then, and for a single, golden moment in late September I have nothing more to wish for. How strange hope is. Promising nothing but still making sense, it hovers here as all around us red and yellow leaves flame in the lowering sun. Strung between plants, fat spiders wait in the gilded bull's-eyes of their webs. David spots a fly, gauze-wrapped and still. The web trembles. "Look," he calls to our boys. As we gather around to look, the last of the light reaches through the trees. It sparks off leaves, off a length of spider silk stretched from one end of the yard to the other; it coats our arms and the spaces between us, suspending us in its amber light, linking leaf to arm, and past to present to future. And so we stand here, held in this moment together.

Acknowledgments

MY GRATITUDE GOES FIRST TO ALL WHO HELPED US HOLD
Silvan in life. This includes the amazing Dr. A, Nurse Kerry and
the rest of the hospital staff, as well as the family, friends, neighbors, acquaintances and even strangers who became part of
his brief life. You know who you are. We did not parent alone and
we are deeply grateful for it.

Nor did I parent this book alone. Going as far back as high
school and college, I am grateful for my teachers Ann Cromey
and Lena Lenček; and later, for the support of established writers:
Michael Cunningham, Tobias Wolff, Al Young, Louis B. Jones,
Lynn Freed. I am grateful to Micheline Marcom for urging me to
keep a diary about Silvan, to Susie Davis and Holly Fleming for
knowing it was time to turn those pages into a book, and to Eve
Müller whose insight shaped not only this book but the very
way I think. I am indebted to Sylvia Brownrigg, brave mother herself, who generously agreed to read the first draft. And to Ayelet
Waldman who sought that first draft out – without your swift
mind and big heart, this book might never have been published.
To the members of my writing group, especially Lindsey Critten-
den and Audrey Ferber, who challenged every whining, bitter
word, forcing me to become a better person through my prose.
For help in ethical research, I thank Rich Gula. For medical exper-
tise, Michael Singer. For general support, more friends than I can

list but especially Eliza Patten, Julia Scheeres, Jenny Pritchett, Laleh Khadivi, Margie Ryan, and Teresa Sharpe.

Of course, all this would mean little without my agent, Mary Evans, who had such faith. As I said when you took me on, if you were the only person ever to be changed by this book, that would have been enough; but how much better that you fiercely believed everyone should have a chance to read it. Thank you. Likewise, to my intrepid editor Rhonda Hughes and to everyone at Hawthorne Books. You all treated my story with respect and compassion, but also with the wisdom of good publishers. Thank you also to Erica Jong who graciously agreed to introduce me to the world.

Finally, I could not have written this book without the support of my family: my parents, my parents-in-law, my brothers and sister, my brothers-and-sisters-in-law. Your warm reception of the book alone has made the project worthwhile. How lucky I am for all of you. And how lucky I am for my children. Miles and Ivan, thank you for your tender interest in your absent brother and for your acceptance that I share my love for you with him. Last but not least, I'm grateful to David with whom I lived this story. Loyal and loving throughout Silvan's life, you have remained steadfast in the birth of this book, debating with bright and fearless honesty, improving what I did not think could be improved. Because of you, Silvan will be remembered well.